DISCIPLING THROUGH GALATIANS

*Verse-by-verse
through the book of Galatians*

Verse-by-verse Meditation
and Discipleship Tool
through the Book of Galatians

Unless otherwise indicated, all Scripture quotations are taken from the *King James Version* of the Bible in the public domain.

Discipling Through Galatians
Copyright © 2012 Andrew Wommack Ministries Inc.

ISBN 13: 978-1-59548-061-3
eBook ISBN 13: 978-1-68031-919-4

Permission is granted to duplicate or reproduce for discipleship purposes on the condition that it is distributed free of charge.

Andrew Wommack Ministries
PO Box 3333
Colorado Springs CO 80934-3333

awmi.net

Introduction to
The Epistle of Paul to the Galatians

Don Krow

Galatia

This letter is addressed to "the churches of Galatia." But what does "Galatia" mean? "Galatia" is the name that was given originally to the territory in north-central Asia Minor, where the invading Gauls settled in the third century before Christ and maintained an independent kingdom for many years. Gradually the Gallic population was absorbed into the other peoples living there, and after a number of political changes, the territory became the property of Rome in 25 B.C. The Romans incorporated this northern section into a larger division of land which they made a province and called by the name of Galatia. Galatia, then under Roman rule, could mean Galatia proper, which the Gauls had founded, or it could be applied to the whole Roman province which included the southern cities of Pisidian Antioch, Iconium, Derbe, and Lystra.

To which of these did Paul refer when he wrote his epistle to the churches of Galatia (Gal. 1:2)? The usage of the New Testament appears in seven passages. In Galatians 1:2 and in 3:1 the people of the churches are addressed, but no hint is given of their location beyond the mere use of the name. In I Corinthians 16:1, Paul spoke of "the churches of Galatia", whom he had asked for a contribution for the poor in Jerusalem. In the same context he referred to Macedonia (16:5), to Achaia (16:15), and to Asia (16:19). Since these last three names refer to Roman provinces, it seems probable that Galatia in the context should also mean the Roman province as a whole (NTS, p. 265).

Two other passages that allude to Galatia are found in Acts 16:6 and Acts 18:23.

The Gauls

"The people for whom the province was named were Gauls, a Celtic tribe from the same stock which inhabited France. They were warlike people and on the move. Their boundaries varied, and for many years they retained their customs and own language. They actually were blond Orientals. These Gallic Celts had much of the same temperament and characteristics as those who came out of Europe or England. Caesar said of them: 'The infirmity of the Gauls is that they are fickle in their resolves, fond of change, and not to be trusted.' In the book of Acts we read that the Galatians wanted to make Paul a god one day, and the next day they stoned him (Acts 14:8-20). Therefore the epistle to the Galatians has a particular message for us because it was written to people who were like us in many ways. They had a like temper, and they were beset on every hand by cults and isms innumerable - which take us, likewise from the gospel of grace." (TTB, pp. 8-9)

Religious Background

"North Galatia resisted Greek-Roman culture, keeping its own gods and Celtic language. South Galatia adopted the cult of emperor worship, and Judaism also persisted there for centuries after Christ" (WILSB, p. 641).

Date of Writing

"At best the date is uncertain. It could have been written early around A.D. 48 or placed during the time of his other great epistles, around A.D. 52-57. A lot depends upon the destination of the letter. There are two main views:

1. The North Galatian theory. This view holds that the letter was written to churches in north-central Asia Minor where the Gauls had settled when they invaded the area in the third century B.C. It is held that Paul visited this area on his second missionary journey, though Acts contains no reference to such a visit. It was written between A.D. 52-57 from Ephesus or Macedonia." (NIVSB).

2. The South Galatian theory. "According to this view Galatians was written to churches in the southern area of the Roman province of Galatia (Pisidian Antioch, Iconium, Lystra and Derbe)—churches that Paul had founded on his first missionary journey. Paul usually concentrated on the great centers of population, where his work would reach the most people. Furthermore, the Judaistic controversy, which caused the letter to be written, would be more apt to reach the nearer cities in the southern part of the province. All in all, the South Galatian theory seems more likely." (NIVSB; ETNT, p. 293)

"That Paul addressed the churches in the south part of Galatia is supported by the following facts: (1) He and Barnabas had visited the cities of Iconium, Lystra, Derbe and Pisidian Antioch, all in south Galatia, and had established churches in the vicinity during the first missionary journey. (For Paul's first missionary journey see Acts 13:1-14:28). (2) Familiar reference to Barnabas (Gal. 2:1,9,13) would be unexplainable in a letter sent to northern Galatia, where Barnabas seems to have been unknown. (3) In the south Galatian cities there were Jews who might have caused the events mentioned in Galatians" (Acts 13:14-51; 14:1-7; 16:1-5 [UBD, p. 386]). (4) "The main roads from Paul's hometown of Tarsus pass directly through the cities of South not North Galatia, the Judaizers were not likely to by pass the southern cities for the northern cities. (5) Representatives of South Galatia accompanied the offering for the poor in Jerusalem but none were from North Galatia (Acts 20:4)" (BKC, p. 588).

"Galatians may have been sent from Antioch around 48 A.D. prior to Paul's visit to Jerusalem to attend the apostolic gathering of Acts 15. If so, Galatians would be the earliest of the apostle's letters" (UBD, p. 386).

The Judaizers

"Throughout history people have 'added on' various requirements to the gospel, almost always with an appeal to scripture. The crime of the Judaizers was not that they substituted something for Christ's work, but rather they tried to add something to it" (WISB; TNTC). "In a way, one can understand their point of view. For centuries, Jews had held to the law as the righteous path to favor with God" (WILSBD, p.642) (Lev. 18:5; Dt. 30:15-20; Mt. 19:16-22; Lk. 10:25,26). "To the Judaizers, Christianity could only be understood in terms of the Old Covenant. When the apostle Peter preached Christ on the Day of Pentecost didn't he preach from the Old Testament prophet Joel (Acts 2:16)? So Christianity was faced with a problem: What has the new to do with the old?

Paul shares the general point of view of his opponents and recognizes the divine authority of the Old Testament in all its parts; but for him the elements of gracious promise in the Old Testament have **permanent** significance, while the law has only a temporary and inferior place in the working out of God's purposes.

Paul shows these Galatians that the faith-promise principle of the Old Testament is as old as Abraham (Gen. 15:6) and that the law was adapted only as a temporary measure until Christ would come (Gal. 3:17-19)" (TBC). Paul states that they have mistaken the actual nature of the law. It may offer blessing and life to all who succeed in keeping it, but it also pronounces a curse on all who do not (Gal. 3:10). Since no one (other than Christ) has ever succeeded in keeping it, justification (right-standing with God) could never come by it (Gal. 2:21). Scripture is clear that it is faith in Christ that puts men in right standing with God and not the works of the law (Gen. 15:6; Gal. 3:11).

"Judaizers were a sect of Jewish Christians who, not willing to accept the teaching of the apostles on this matter (Acts 15), continued to insist that Christians must come to God through the law, and keep the Jewish law of Moses.

They made it their business to visit and unsettle and trouble Gentile Churches. They were simply determined to stamp Christ with the Jewish Trademark.

Against this Paul stood adamant. Had the observance of the Law been imposed on Gentile converts, Paul's whole gospel and lifework would have been in vain" (HBH, p. 609).

"The expansion of Christianity from a Jewish sect into a World Religion was Paul's consuming passion, in pursuit of which he broke every hindering tie, and strained every faculty of mind and body for upwards of thirty years" (HBH).

The effort to Judaize the Gentile Churches was brought to an end by the fall of Jerusalem, A.D. 70, which "severed all relation between Judaism and Christianity. Up to this time, Christianity was regarded as a Sect or Branch of Judaism. But from then on Jews and Christians were apart. A small sect of Jewish Christians, the Ebionites, remained, in decreasing numbers, for two centuries, hardly recognized by the general Church, and regarded as Apostates by their own race" (HBH, p. 609).

In some respects, as a foreigner may become a citizen of our country, to the Judaizers a Gentile might become a Christian through faith in Christ, circumcision, and observance of the law.

Galatians Outline

Greetings (Gal. 1:1-5)

This new "gospel" is no gospel (Gal. 1:6-10)

Paul received his commission directly from Christ (Gal. 1:11-17)

Paul's first visit to Jerusalem after his conversion (Gal. 1:18-24)

Paul's second visit to Jerusalem (Gal. 2:1-10)

Why Paul opposed Peter at Antioch (Gal. 2:11-21)

An appeal to their own experience (Gal. 3:1-14)

Law and promise (Gal. 3:15-22)

Christians are full-grown sons of God (Gal. 3:23-29)

Going back to infancy (Gal. 4:1-7)

Going back to slavery (Gal. 4:8-11)

A further personal appeal (Gal. 4:12-20)

Freedom, not bondage (Gal. 4:21-5:1)

Grace, not law (Gal. 5:2-12)

Liberty, not license (Gal. 5:13-26)

A call to mutual aid (Gal. 6:1-5)

Sowing and reaping (Gal. 6:6-10)

Paul takes up the pen (Gal. 6:11)

False and true boasting (Gal. 6:12-16)

The true marks of a servant of Christ (Gal. 6:17)

Benediction (Gal. 6:18)

(NBD, p. 447)

Chart of Early Pauline Events

Event	Reference	Time
Resurrection; Pentecost	Acts 1:3,5; 2:1	A.D. 29
Conversion of Paul at Damascus	Acts 9:1-18; 22:3-21	31
Visit to Arabia Return to Damascus	Gal. 1:17	
Paul's first visit to Jerusalem Interview with Cephas Spent 15 days in the city	Gal. 1:18	33
Departure to Syria and Cilicia Early ministry in Antioch	Gal. 1:21	
Second visit to Jerusalem Motivated by revelation Private interview Complaint about "False Brethren" Agreement with James, Cephas, & John about the Gospel	Gal. 2:1-10	46
Paul's first Missionary Journey Return to Antioch Visit of Cephas Controversy Writing of Galatians	Gal. 2:11	48
Council of Jerusalem	Acts 15:1-35	48/49

About the Author of the Letter to the Galatians

PAUL - Wrote 14 epistles in the New Testament. His Jewish name was Saul, meaning "asked", and his Roman name was Paul, meaning "little" or "small". His name Paul was used for the first time in Acts 13:9. He may have been a small person or he may have wanted to be known as the small one in God's service. It was the name of Jesus that he wanted to be magnified.

BORN: In Tarsus, a city of Cilicia (Acts 21:39; 22:3).

DESCENT: A Hebrew, of Jewish descent, from the tribe of Benjamin (Phil.3:5).

RELIGION: Judaism, from the sect called the Pharisees (Acts 23:6). [See note 4 at Lk. 6:7, p. 162-LFT for more information.] A leader in Judaism, a possible member of the Sanhedrin who gave his vote against the Christians in Acts 26:10. [See note 11 at Mt. 5:22, p. 128-LFT for information about the Sanhedrin].

EDUCATION: Educated in the law, learning the Hebrew language and Scriptures. At 12 years of age he was sent to Jerusalem to learn the law at the feet of Gamaliel (Acts 22:3). He was also acquainted with Aramaic Greek which was the language of Tarsus, and he possibly knew a little Latin.

CITIZENSHIP: Paul had inherited the rights of Roman citizenship (Acts 22:28). "This privilege had been granted, or descended to his father, as an individual right, perhaps for some services rendered to Caesar during the civil wars" (Conybeare and Howson; Bloomfield, NT).

OCCUPATION: A Tentmaker (Acts 18:3).

HIS ZEAL FOR THE LAW - A PERSECUTOR: We first hear of Saul at the martyrdom of Stephen. Saul was probably in his twenties at the time (Acts 7:58). Saul "entered into every house (Acts 8:3), and those whom he tore from their homes he committed to prison. Not only men but women also suffered at his hands. These persecuted people were even scourged in the synagogues (Acts 26:11), nor was Stephen the only one to suffer death (Acts 22:4; 26:10). Saul even endeavored to make them blaspheme God (Acts 26:11). He did much evil to Christ's saints (Acts 9:13). When the church at Jerusalem was scattered by persecution Saul persecuted them even to strange cities (Acts 26:11; cp. Acts 8:3; Gal. 1:13; 1 Tim. 1:13). He also went to the high priest and desired letters to Damascus where he had reason to believe that Christians may be found" (UBD).

SAUL'S CONVERSION: It appears that Paul's conversion took place while he was in this thirties. We think that Paul was about 10 years younger than Jesus Christ. After meeting Jesus Christ on the Damascus road he neither ate nor drank for three days but sought God in prayer (Acts 9:9,11). He was immediately baptized (Acts 9:18; 22:16) and preached Christ in the synagogues saying, "He is the Son of God" (Acts 9:20).

PAUL'S MISSIONARY JOURNEYS: "It is clear from Acts 13:1-21:17 that Paul went on three missionary journeys. There is also reason to believe that he made a fourth journey after his release from the Roman imprisonment recorded in Acts 28. The conclusion that such a journey did indeed take place is based on: (1) Paul's declared intention to go to Spain (Rom. 15:23-25), (2). . . the implication that Paul was released following his first Roman imprisonment, and (3) statements in early Christian literature that he took the gospel as far as Spain" (NIVSB, p. 1836).

PAUL'S DEATH: "After Paul's release from prison in Rome (Acts 28) and after his fourth missionary journey, during which he wrote 1 Timothy and Titus, Paul was again imprisoned under Emperor Nero" (NIVSB, p. 1843). "While he was a prisoner, he wrote his second epistle to Timothy, in which he both mentions his first defence and his impending death. . ."(Eusebius, *Ecclesiastical History*, 2.22.2-3). History says that Paul's martyrdom took place in Rome by beheading (2 Tim. 4:6-8).

WHY LOOK AT VARIOUS TRANSLATIONS?

Although I personally adhere to the "Textus Receptus" or "Received Text" which is the foundation for the King James Version, The New King James Version, Young's Literal Translation, etc., why not use a full set of tools for our biblical studies? A Greek word may require several or even several dozen English words to render it adequately. The Greek scholar A.T. Robertson points out one reason for this: "Language was originally pictographic...Words have never gotten wholly away from the picture stage...There is no single Greek word that has an EXACT equivalent in a single English word" [*A Beginner's Reader-Grammar for N.T. Greek*]. "To adequately render some Greek words often requires so many words that we end up not with a strict translation but actually with a sort of translation plus commentary, or paraphrase, on the Greek text which is usually quite awkward for use as a standard English Bible" [*How to Use N.T. Greek Study Aids*, p. 26].

No translation can ever hope to reproduce completely all the shades of meaning found in the Greek New Testament. As Kenneth Wuest points out: "In a translation which keeps to a minimum of words, that is, where one English word for instance is the translation of one Greek word, it is impossible for the translator to bring out all the shades of meaning in the Greek word" [Untranslatable Riches from the Greek N.T.].

This is why I have sought in this commentary effort to use the various translations and paraphrases available to help build and see a complete picture of that which the apostle Paul was trying to portray in his epistle to the Galatians. The primary reason for a translation in the first place is to help readers to understand God's Word. I have sought to use the Authorized King James Version as the foundation of our study and to use the various translations and pharaphrases as a kind of commentary on the passage. Keep in mind that there are about three different kinds of translations: (1) A "Literal" translation, seeking a word-for-word rendering of the original text. Translations such as these are the King James Version, The New American Standard Version, The New King James Version, Young's Literal Translation, etc. (2) "Free" translating. This is the translators' attempt to create the same sense or content of the original, but not necessarily the same grammatical form or closeness of words. Some translations that use this approach are the New International Version, The New Jerusalem Bible, Today's English Version, etc. (3) A "Paraphrase." A paraphrase is not a true translation but is more like hearing a preacher preach or teach about a passage. It's in the writer's own words and not the wording or form of the original Greek. It is more like reading a commentary than an actual translation. The most popular paraphrase of today is Kenneth Taylor's, The Living Bible.

By reading various translations I believe a person will acquire a fuller understanding of the thought and content of the original Greek.

Don Krow

Galatians 1:1-24
Discipleship Commentary

. . . .

Galatians 1:1
  Paul, an apostle, (not of men, neither by man, but by Jesus Christ, and God the Father, who raised him from the dead;) (KJV)

  Paul, an apostle (not from men nor through man, but through Jesus Christ and God the Father who raised Him from the dead), (NKJV)

  From: Paul the missionary and all the other Christians here. To: The churches of Galatia. I was not called to be a missionary by any group or agency. My call is from Jesus Christ himself, and from God the Father who raised him from the dead. (LB)

  This letter is from Paul. I am a missionary sent by Jesus Christ and God the Father Who raised Jesus from the dead. I am not sent by men or by any one man. (TNLT)

  (Gal. 1: 1-5) If you notice in the King James Version, the first five verses in chapter 1 make up one complete sentence. This is in accordance with the first-century Jewish and Greek tradition of writing letters, which included the name of the author, a short reference to the recipients, and some customary words of greetings. The usual practice of Paul would be to express thanksgiving, prayer, and praise for the saints within his salutation (1 Cor. 1:1-5, Phil. 1:1-5, Col. 1:1-4, 1 Thess. 1:1-3, 2 Thess. 1:1-3, and 2 Tim. 1:1-3). In this letter to the Galatians, Paul does not follow his normal course but rather immediately defends his apostleship, omits thanksgiving and prayer, and begins to exhibit a mood of almost anger at what is happening to the Galatian believers.

  (Gal. 1:1) The name "Paul" is a Roman name that means "small" or "little." It is first used in Acts 13:9. It was probably the name used to identify him more closely with the Gentiles. Paul could have been a small person in stature, or he may have wanted to identify himself as small in comparison to the magnified name of Jesus, the name which he was preaching.
  The word "apostle" is a translation of the Greek word "apostolos," meaning "apo"—"from" and "stello"—"to send," thus referring to the act of sending someone on a commission to represent the sender. It was used of a messenger who was provided with credentials. Our word "ambassador" would be a good translation (*Wuest Word Studies in Greek, Volume I*, p. 28). It is important that Paul defend his apostleship, for if the false teachers called the Judaizers could discredit his apostleship, they would also discredit the message he was preaching. To make this point of apostleship more forceful, the German Common Language Translation translates this phrase as "Paul, an apostle, writes this letter."

Paul's apostleship was not bestowed upon him from the earthly Jesus as the other apostles' was (Matt. 10:1-5), but his commission was from the resurrected Lord Jesus Christ who was raised the Son of God in power (Rom. 1:4).

Notice that Jesus Christ and God the Father are on a par of equality in bestowing Paul's apostleship. Paul further makes it clear that no group or agency of man had sent him.

Galatians 1:2

And all the brethren which are with me, unto the churches of Galatia: (KJV)

From Paul to the churches of Galatia, and from all the brothers who are here with me, (TJB)

And all the Christians who are with me, to the churches in Galatia (Beck)

(Gal. 1:2) In Paul's greeting, he mentions "all the brethren which are with me." Although Paul is the composer of this letter, he is relating the fact that he is not alone in stating the doctrinal truths that he will portray in this letter. There is an "amen" from many as to what Paul will be sharing with these Galatians.

Notice that Paul uses the plural "churches" in addressing the Galatians. This was a circular letter that is not going to a city but rather to a Roman province. There were four major cities in this province: Antioch Pisidia, Iconium, Lystra, and Derbe.

Galatians 1:3

Grace be to you and peace from God the Father, and from our Lord Jesus Christ, (KJV)

So I greet you with great words, grace and peace. (TM)

(Gal. 1:3) It's almost amusing that within Paul's salutation, he says, "Grace be to you... [FROM GOD]." He is writing this letter, because the Galatians have started to fall away from the principles of grace (Gal. 5:4). He is now stating within his greeting that the source of grace is God. So who is legalism from?

Notice that grace is from God the Father and from our Lord Jesus Christ. "The law was given by Moses, but grace and truth came by Jesus Christ" (John 1:17).

"Our Lord Jesus Christ" indicates that He is our Master (Lord), our Savior (Jesus), and our Messiah (Christ). Within the New Covenant, He has become ours and we have become His, very much like a marriage relationship (Rom. 7:4). Second Corinthians 6:16 states that within the New Covenant, God says, "I will be [THEIR GOD], and they shall be [MY PEOPLE]."

Galatians 1:4

Who gave himself for our sins, that he might deliver us from this present evil world, according to the will of God and our Father: (KJV)

Who gave (yielded) Himself up [to atone] for our sins (and to save and sanctify us), in order to rescue and deliver us from this present wicked age and world order, in accordance with the will and purpose and plan of our God and Father. (AMP)

We know the meaning of those words because Jesus Christ rescued us from this evil world we're in by offering Himself as a sacrifice for our sins. God's plan is that we all experience that rescue. (TM)

(Gal. 1:4) Now Paul is stating that Jesus gave Himself for our sins, not only that we might be justified, but also "that he might deliver us from this present evil world." The same Greek word for "deliver" is "exaireo" and it is used in Acts 12:11 for Peter's deliverance out of the hand of Herod (Acts 12:1-11) and also in Acts 23:27 of Paul's rescue from the narrow escape of death by the Jews (Acts 21:20-36). The point is that the Gospel of grace is a "rescue" and "deliverance" out of the hand of sin (Rom. 6:6, 8:2). The Gospel has been given "to set us free so that we do not have to live like people do in this present evil age" (*UBS Handbook*, p. 9). This is "according to the will of God and our Father."

Galatians 1:5

To whom be glory for ever and ever. Amen. (KJV)

All glory to God through all the ages of eternity. Amen. (LB)

(Gal. 1:5) If you really understand the Gospel you shall break out in praise!

Galatians 1:6

I marvel that ye are so soon removed from him that called you into the grace of Christ unto another gospel: (KJV)

I am amazed that you are turning away so soon from God who, in his love and mercy, invited you to share the eternal life he gives through Christ; you are already following a different "way to heaven," which really doesn't go to heaven at all. (LB)

I am astonished that you are so quickly deserting the one who called you by the grace of Christ and are turning to a different gospel (NIV)

I am surprised at you! In no time at all you are deserting the one who called you by the grace of Christ, and are accepting another gospel. (TEV)

(Gal. 1:6) The Greek word translated "marvel" in this verse is "thaumazo" and carries the idea of that which would "evoke surprise." It is translated in various translations by the phrases "I marvel," "I am amazed," "I am astonished," and "I am surprised at you!" (KJV, LB, NIV, and TEV). Why? Not because they were deserting some doctrine of theology but because they were deserting GOD HIMSELF. Whenever a person removes himself from the grace that's revealed in Christ, he removes himself from God Himself. In the Greek, the removing is in the present tense, which indicates that the removing is in progress, but is not yet complete. In other words, the Galatians were in a state of double-mindedness, with their ears turned toward a false gospel.

Galatians 1:7

Which is not another; but there be some that trouble you, and would pervert the gospel of Christ. (KJV)

There is actually no other true gospel. However, some people are disturbing you; they want to distort the gospel of Christ. (SE)

Which is really no gospel at all. Evidently some people are throwing you into confusion and are trying to pervert the gospel of Christ. (NIV)

For there is no other way than the one we showed you; you are being fooled by those who twist and change the truth concerning Christ. (LB)

(Gal. 1:7) Paul is now saying that the Galatians are turning toward "another" gospel. There are two different Greek words used in verses 6 and 7 for the word "another." In verse 6 the Greek word for "another" is "heteros" and means "another of a DIFFERENT kind." That's why the New International Version translates this phrase as "turning to a [DIFFERENT GOSPEL]." The Greek adjective used in verse 7 for "another" is "allos" and means "another of the SAME kind." The Galatians were not turning toward a gospel that was similar in nature to the one they had already received but were turning to a totally different gospel, which verse 7 states "is really no gospel at all" (NIV).

To illustrate this, imagine that I had two apples—one that stood for the Gospel of grace, the other that stood for the gospel that the Judaizers preached. Then I said, "Receive the gospel of the Judaizers" and handed you a banana. I have just offered you a gospel of a totally different nature, which Paul said is not the Gospel at all.

Notice that Paul says, "that some are TROUBLING you, DISTURBING you, and throwing you into CONFUSION" (KJV, SE, and NIV). How? By PERVERTING, TWISTING, CHANGING, and DISTORTING the Gospel of Christ, i.e., the good news about Christ (KJV, LB, and SE). The Greek word for "perverting" the Gospel means "to change" the Gospel, not by denying it, but by mixing something with it. The Galatians were doing this in at least five different ways: (1) They tried to find favor with God by observing special days (Sabbaths), months, seasons, and years (Gal. 4:10). (2) They were making circumcision mandatory along with belief in Jesus for salvation (Gal. 5:2 [LB]). (3) They thought that part of their righteousness came through observing the Law (Gal. 5:4). (4) They believed that righteousness could be obtained by the strength and ability of their own flesh (Gal. 3:3). (5) They also believed in Jesus as Messiah and Savior (Acts 15:5). As long as these things (i.e., points 1-4) are voluntary, they are not a perversion of the Gospel (Rom. 14:1-6). But if they become an obligation as a means of obtaining righteousness (justification), at that point the Gospel is perverted.

We could also say that stating, "Pray, fast, go to church, read your Bible, tithe, and believe in Jesus and you will be accepted in God's sight" would be a perversion of the Gospel. If doing those things were merely a voluntary matter, it would be good and well-pleasing to God, and we should do those things. But if it's mandatory to receive righteousness (justification) before God, it perverts the truth (Gal. 2:21). God has designed salvation in such a way that there will never be boasting from man's flesh (Rom. 3:27-28).

Galatians 1:8

But though we, or an angel from heaven, preach any other gospel unto you than that which we have preached unto you, let him be accursed. (KJV)

But even if we or an angel from heaven should preach to you a gospel that is different from the one we preached to you, may he be condemned to hell! (TEV)

Let God's curses fall on anyone, including myself, who preaches any other way to be saved than the one we told you about; yes, if an angel comes from heaven and preaches any other message, let him be forever cursed. (LB)

(Gal. 1:8) Paul is now stating "though we," the apostles or companions with Paul in preaching, "or an angel from heaven," claiming an added revelation to the Gospel of Christ, preach any gospel unto them than that which Paul had originally preached to them, let those messengers be accursed. The counterparts for this word in the Hebrew meant, "To be appointed to utter destruction and to be completely destroyed." These words were used in Numbers 21:3 of the children of Israel utterly destroying the Canaanites, and also in Joshua 6:16-17 of the city of Jericho and it's inhabitants being an accursed thing unto the Lord and appointed to utter destruction.

Paul is now stressing the importance of preaching the true message of the Gospel of

Christ. If anyone tampers with the true message of the Gospel of grace, Paul states, "Let him be accursed!" The Greek word is anathema" and, again, means, "a person or thing doomed to destruction" (Thayer's Greek Lexicon). The Today's English Version translates this, "May he be condemned to hell!" This statement will certainly be true of those who have turned away from the good news of Jesus unto another way of salvation, which is to be without a Gospel at all.

Galatians 1:9

As we said before, so say I now again, If any man preach any other gospel unto you than that ye have received, let him be accursed. (KJV)

Let me repeat what I have just said: If anyone shall proclaim to you a gospel different from what you have received, let there be a curse on him! (NOR)

As we said before, I will say it again. If any man is preaching another good news to you which is not the one you have received, let him be kept from being with Christ. (TNLT)

(Gal. 1:9) Paul is reinforcing the statement he had just made. "I said it once, and I WILL SAY IT AGAIN: If anyone preaches a GOSPEL TO YOU THAT IS DIFFERENT, let him be 'anathema' (eternally condemned)."

With the hundreds of religions and gospels that are being preached, it behooves us to return to the original Gospel as recorded in the Scripture. The book of Acts records 13 messages that the apostles preached and the response that was demanded. Many times these messages have been the standard by which I've tested a person's gospel. Books such as Romans and Galatians then expound on and expand that message.

Galatians 1:10

For do I now persuade men, or God? or do I seek to please men? for if I yet pleased men, I should not be the servant of Christ. (KJV)

I am not trying to please people. I want to please God. Do you think I am trying to please people? If I were doing that, I would not be a servant of Christ. (CEV)

Do you think I'm now trying to win man over? No! God is the One whom I am trying to please. Am I trying to please man? If I were, I would not be a servant of Christ. (SE)

Now, am I trying to win the favor of men, or of God? Do I seek to be a man-pleaser? If I were still seeking popularity with men, I should not be a bondservant of Christ, the Messiah. (AMP)

(Gal. 1:10) Paul is stating, "I'm not preaching man's gospel. I'm not trying to please man." The word for "persuade" in the King James is "peitho" and means "to win over, and render friendly to one's self" (*Wuest Word Studies in the Greek, Volume I*, p. 42). Paul was not trying to win over and make friends by preaching man's gospel. If that were the case, he would not be the servant of Christ. Paul states in 1 Thessalonians 2:4, "We speak as messengers from God, trusted by him to tell the truth; we change his message not one bit to suit the taste of those who hear it; for we serve God alone, who examines our hearts' deepest thoughts" (LB).

As a "servant" Paul can have only one master, and he has chosen Christ (Matt. 6:24). Therefore, he will speak only the message of the one he serves.

Galatians 1:11

But I certify you, brethren, that the gospel which was preached of me is not after man. (KJV)

But I make known to you, brethren, that the gospel which was preached by me is not according to man. (NKJV)

I want you to know, brothers, that the gospel I preached is not something that man made up. (NIV)

Brothers, I am letting you know that the gospel which I preached to you was not man-made. (SE)

Let me tell you, my brothers, that the gospel I preach is not of human origin. (TEV)

(Gal. 1:11) Paul now states, "But I certify you brethren [a phrase that means 'to make known, i.e., to make it perfectly clear'] that the gospel which was preached of me ['preached' being a verb and often rendered in a way that indicates a continuous action, i.e., the gospel which I am in a custom of preaching] is not after man, it's not according to man, it's not something that man made up, it's not man-made, it's not of human origin" (KJV, NKJV, NIV, SE, and TEV).

Galatians 1:12

For I neither received it of man, neither was I taught it, but by the revelation of Jesus Christ. (KJV)

I didn't receive it through the traditions, and I wasn't taught it in some school. I got it straight from God, received the message directly from Jesus Christ. (TM)

No man gave it to me, no man taught it to me; it came to me as a direct revelation from Jesus Christ. (J.B. Phillips)

For I neither received it from man, nor was I taught it, but I received it through a revelation of Jesus Christ. (NASV)

(Gal. 1:12) Paul did not receive his Gospel from a human being, neither did he learn it from a human source, but it was revealed to him by Jesus Christ. The Greek meaning of a "revelation" of Jesus Christ carries the idea of "taking off a cover, i.e. an unveiling or disclosure" of Jesus Christ. It wasn't that Paul had no understanding of the historical facts that Jesus had died, but now he had a spiritual understanding of the historical facts that revealed that salvation was through Jesus alone.

The little preposition "of," i.e., the revelation OF Jesus Christ could mean two things: (1) The revelation of the Gospel was FROM Jesus Christ to Paul. (2) The content of the revelation, which was from God, WAS JESUS CHRIST (*UBS Handbook*, p. 18 [Rom. 1:1-3]).

Galatians 1:13

For ye have heard of my conversation in time past in the Jew's religion, how that beyond measure I persecuted the church of God, and wasted it: (KJV)

You know what I was like when I followed the Jewish religion—how I went after the Christians mercilessly, hunting them down and doing my best to get rid of them all. (LB)

For you heard of my manner of life aforetime in Judaism, that beyond measure I kept on continuously persecuting the Church of God and continuously bringing destruction upon it. (N.T. AET)

You know how I used to live as a Jew. I was cruel to God's church and even tried to destroy it. (CEV)

You have heard of my old life when I followed the Jewish religion. I made it as hard as I could for the Christians and did everything I could to destroy the Christian church. (TNLT)

(Gal. 1:13) The Galatians had heard about Paul's former conduct and manner of life in Judaism (how they heard we are not sure: word of mouth, from Paul himself, etc.). The phrase "in time past" refers to his former life before meeting Jesus Christ. Paul's religious zeal is referred to in Philippians 3:5-6, which describes him as a "Hebrew of the Hebrews. . . [as] touching the righteousness which is in the law, blameless," (KJV). That is, he "tried to obey every Jewish rule and regulation right down to the very last point" (LB). He was in a religious system, like all of the world's religious systems that have tried to achieve righteousness before God by human effort. When confronted by the claims of Jesus Christ and the real truth proclaimed in the law, he realized he was the chief of sinners (1 Tim. 1:15), that by the works of law no person could ever be justified (Gal. 2:16), and that the Gospel was a Gospel of grace (Acts 15:11, 20:24).

Notice that his religious zeal led to the persecuting of those preaching the Gospel of grace. Paul will speak more about this later in his epistle through the illustration of Ishmael and Isaac (Gal.4:21-31). False religion has always persecuted true religion, and it will continue to be this way until the end of the age. Law and grace are two different ways of approaching God, with opposite results (Rom. 9:30-33 - 10:1-10). They're not two different ways of receiving the same thing.

In the Greek, the imperfect tense is used of both words "persecuted" and "wasted." This implies the persecution that Saul persecuted the church with was consistent, in excess, without mercy and continued for some time. The imperfect tense of the verb for "wasted it" indicates an ATTEMPT, as well as an ACTION to "destroy" the church which continued for a period of time (*UBS Handbook*, p. 19).

Galatians 1:14

And profited in the Jew's religion above many my equals in mine own nation, being more exceedingly zealous of the traditions of my fathers. (KJV)

I was one of the most religious Jews of my own age in the whole country, and tried as hard as I possibly could to follow all the old, traditional rules of my religion. (LB)

I was so enthusiastic about the traditions of my ancestors that I advanced head and shoulders above my peers in my career. (TM)

(Gal. 1:14) Paul advanced within the ranks of Judaism. In the Greek, the word for "profited" literally means "to drive forward (as if by beating) i.e., (figuratively and intransitively) to advance" (Strong). Just as in a race, a man might beat an animal to drive him forward and cause him to advance over the others, so Paul was driven by religion. Paul is now speaking of his youth when he advanced and drove himself forward in the Jewish religion beyond many of his own age (Acts 22:3). He was superabundantly zealous for the traditions of men. This would be a good definition for religion: "to make the Word of God of none effect through tradition" (Mark 7:9-13, NIV).

Galatians 1:15-17

But when it pleased God, who separated me from my mother's womb, and called me by his grace, To reveal his Son in me, that I might preach him among the heathen; immediately I conferred not with flesh and blood: Neither went I up to Jerusalem to them which were apostles before me; but I went into Arabia, and returned again unto Damascus. (KJV)

But the God who had set me apart from my very birth called me by his grace, and when he chose to reveal his Son to me, that I might preach him to the Gentiles, instead of consulting with any human being, instead of going up to Jerusalem to those who had been apostles before me, I went off at once to Arabia, and on my return I came back to Damascus. (MOF)

But then something happened! For even before I was born God had chosen me to be His, and called me—what kindness and grace—To reveal His Son within me so that I could go to the Gentiles and show them the Good News about Jesus. When all this happened to me I didn't go at once and talk it over with anyone else; I didn't go up to Jerusalem to consult with those who were apostles before I was. No, I went away into the deserts of Arabia, and then came back to the city of Damascus. (LB)

Even then God had designs on me. Why, when I was still in my mother's womb He chose and called me out of sheer generosity! How he has intervened and revealed His Son to me so that I might joyfully tell non-Jews about Him. Immediately after my calling – without consulting anyone around me and without going up to Jerusalem to confer with those who were apostle's long before I was – I got away to Arabia. (TM)

(Gal. 1:15-17) If you notice in the English as well as in the Greek text, verses 15-17 are one complete sentence.

Paul is speaking about three things that God's grace has done for him: (1) He was separated from his mother's womb, i.e., he was set apart and kept apart for a specific purpose from before his birth (Judg. 16:17, Luke 1:13-15). He was set apart to be an apostle. (2) He was "called" by God's grace. The word literally means "to shout at." God's grace shouted at Saul and said, "Turn around, because I want you." (3) It revealed God's Son to him, or in him. It was to show him who God's Son really is. Again, the word "reveal" from Greek means "to take off the cover." What began as God's Son being revealed *to* Paul ended up being a revelation of God's Son *in* Paul (TNTC, p. 52).

This was all the work of grace that Paul "might preach Him [Jesus] among the Gentiles." This revelation was for the purpose of proclamation. It was a revelation of God's Son—an illumination of Christ that required no conference, no communication, no consulting from flesh and blood, i.e., a living person.

In verse 17, Paul now states what he didn't do and what he did do. He didn't go to Jerusalem to consult with the 12 original apostles about the Gospel. What he did do was go into the deserts of Arabia (maybe to study the Old Testament scriptures without tradition) and then return back to the city of Damascus.

Galatians 1:18-19

Then after three years I went up to Jerusalem to see Peter, and abode with him fifteen days. But other of the apostles saw I none, save James the Lord's brother. (KJV)

Then three years later I went up to Jerusalem to become acquainted with Cephas, and stayed with him fifteen days. But I did not see any other of the apostles except James the Lord's brother. (NASB)

Later I returned to Damascus, but it was three years before I went up to Jerusalem to compare stories with Peter. I was there only fifteen days – but what days they were! Except for our Master's brother James, I saw no other apostles. (I'm telling you the absolute truth in this.) (TM)

(Gal. 1:18-19) Paul mentioning the three years here, is probably referring to the thought that three years after his conversion, he went up to Jerusalem. The reason for this visit was to get acquainted with Peter. He stayed with Peter for 15 days. There may be two reasons that Paul mentions this visit: (1) He was only with Peter a brief period of time and could not have possibly been instructed fully in the Gospel so quickly. The Judiazers were saying that Paul had learned his Gospel from the apostles and had now defected from its original message. Paul's point continues to be that the Gospel was revealed to him not by man. (2) The Judiazers could claim that Paul's message was not that of Peter's, and Paul wants his readers to understand his acquaintance and harmony with Peter and James the brother of the Lord, the overseer of the Jerusalem church.

It could be also possible that because of persecution from the Jews, Paul's visit was cut short (Acts 9:27-30, 22:17-21).

The James mentioned in verse 19 is not James the son of Zebedee or James the son of Alphaeus, part of the original 12 (Matt. 10:1-4), but James the brother of the Lord, who is also referred to as an apostle in this verse.

Galatians 1:20

Now the things which I write unto you, behold, before God, I lie not. (KJV)

(Listen to what I am saying, for I am telling you this in the very presence of God. This is exactly what happened—I am not lying to you.) (LB)

(Gal. 1:20) Paul wants to strengthen the points of his letter by stating that before God, he is not lying, i.e., he is telling the truth. But obviously someone indeed is lying to the Galatians. If Paul's character or apostleship is questioned, so is his message. Paul speaks about those that say one thing and do another in Romans 2:21-24 and states that inconsistency in character while preaching God's message causes others to think less of God. God is judged by the conduct of those who proclaim His message. Paul states, "Listen to me, what I've written to you is the truth. Before God, I lie not."

Galatians 1:21-22

Afterwards I came into the regions of Syria and Cilicia; And was unknown by face unto the churches of Judaea which were in Christ: (KJV)

Then after this visit I went to Syria and Cilicia. (LB)

I was personally unknown to the churches of Judea that are in Christ. (NIV)

(Gal. 1:21-22) After 15 days with Peter, Paul left Judea and traveled to the Roman provinces of Syria and Cilicia. He was personally unacquainted with the churches of Judea.

The phrase "which were in Christ" distinguishes the Jewish Christians from the Jews and their synagogues in Judea.

Galatians 1:23-24

But they had heard only, That he which persecuted us in times past now preacheth the faith which once he destroyed. And they glorified God in me. (KJV)

They only knew by hearsay, The man who used to persecute us is now preaching the faith he once tried to destroy, and they praised God for what he had done in me. (Knox)

All they knew was what people were saying, that "our former enemy is now preaching the very faith he tried to wreck." And they gave glory to God because of me. (LB)

There was only this report: "That man who once persecuted us is now preaching the very message he used to try to destroy." Their response was to recognize and worship *God* because of *me*. (TM)

(Gal. 1:23-24) The Judean churches kept constantly hearing from others about Paul. HEARD is in the Greek text THEY KEPT CONSTANTLY HEARING (*Wuest's Word Studies in Greek, Volume I*, p. 55). The content of that which they heard was that one who tried to stop people from believing in Christ and destroy the Christian faith is now preaching faith in Christ as the only means of salvation.

In verse 24 "the preposition 'in' is used here as indicating the REASON or BASIS of an action, i.e. 'they praised God for what he had done in me (Paul)'" (Knox, *UBS Handbook*, p. 26). The verb used for "glorified" indicates CONTINUOUS ACTION, i.e., Paul's example caused the Judean churches to continually glorify God. The Living Bible states, "And they gave glory to God because of me."

Galatians 1:1-24
Discipleship Questions

. . . .

1. Read Galatians 1:1. What was Paul's purpose in emphasizing Who had called him to be a messenger for Jesus Christ? _____

2. Read John 15:16. Did you choose Christ? _____

3. What two things did Christ do for you?
   1. _____
   2. _____

4. What was His purpose in choosing you? _____

5. If you accept the calling of the Lord upon your life, what is the result of the fruit you bear? _____

6. Read John 15:16. What does the Lord promise you at the end of this verse? _____

7. Read Acts 20:24. How did Paul view his life and purpose in life? _____

8. Read Romans 5:1-2 (AMP). **"Therefore, since we are justified (acquitted, declared righteous, and given a right standing with God) through faith, let us [grasp the fact that we] have [the peace of reconciliation to hold and to enjoy] peace with God through our Lord Jesus Christ (the Messiah, the Anointed One). 2) Through Him also we have [our] access (entrance, introduction) by faith into this grace (state of God's favor) in which we [firmly and safely] stand. And let us rejoice and exult in our hope of experiencing and enjoying the glory of God."**
According to Romans 5:1, is your "justification by faith" something you earn and are still trying to attain? _____

9. Read Romans 5:1. What is the result of your justification? _____

10. In Romans 5:2, what else do you have access to by your faith? _____

11. What is your current posture in God's grace supposed to be according to Romans 5:2?
    A. Firmly and safely standing.
    B. Faltering and barely hanging on.
    C. Just missed it by a hair.

12. Read Galatians 1:4. What was the purpose for Christ dying on the cross for our sins?
    _____

13. Read Galatians 1:4. Whose plan was it that Christ should die in your place? _____

14. According to Galatians 1:4, can we be delivered, or rescued, from this "present evil world" by any other means? _____

15. According to the quote from the USB Handbook for Galatians 1:4, we have been given grace and peace "so that we do not have to live like people do in this present evil age." If you deny this grace and peace from God, you are essentially saying…
    A. Christ died in vain (Gal. 2:21).
    B. The Word of God is of no effect (Mark 7:13).
    C. Both.

16. Read Galatians 1:5. Who is to receive the glory for our justification and salvation?
    _____

17. Read Galatians 1:6. The error of the Galatians was not just a minor infraction. What was Paul "marveling" over? _____
    _____

18. Read Galatians 1:6. What happens when you deny the grace of God that comes through Jesus Christ? _____

19. Read Galatians 1:6. What were the people turning to and following?
    _____

20. Can you recognize any area of your own life where you have held on to the traditions of men while mixing it with the Gospel? _____
    _____

21. If so, can you now see how any perversion of the true Gospel negates grace and peace?
    _____

22. Read Galatians 1:7. Was the "new gospel" being preached merely a slight shading of the truth? _____

23. Read Acts 4:12. Is there any other way to heaven besides having faith in Jesus Christ?
    _____

24. Are there still people today who are deceived and pervert the truth causing confusion among those seeking to follow Christ? _____ Can you name an example? _____
    _____
    _____

25. Read Galatians 1:8. Is preaching a twisted gospel a serious violation of the truth?
    _____

26. Read Galatians 1:8. Is anyone on earth or in heaven exempt from this potential curse?
    _____

27. Read Galatians 1:3. What was the Gospel that had already been preached?
    _____

28. Have you ever been so emphatic about something that you repeated yourself several times?
    _____

29. What was your purpose in doing so? _____

30. Read Galatians 1:9. How important did Paul feel it was to not distort the Gospel?
    _____

31. Read Galatians 1:10. Was Paul out to win a popularity contest? _____

32. According to Galatians 1:10, what was Paul's primary motivation in rebuking these Christians? _____
    _____

33. What is your motive in sharing the Gospel? _____
    _____

34. Read 2 Timothy 4:2-4. What is the first charge given here?
    _____

35. According to 2 Timothy 4:2, what three things are we also instructed to do when preaching the Word of God?
    1. _____
    2. _____
    3. _____

36. Read 2 Timothy 4:2. How is the Word of God to be delivered?
    With _____
    and _____

37. Regardless if you always speak the truth, will all men always agree with you? _____

38. Read 1 Thessalonians 2:4-6. When Paul preached the Gospel, whose approval did he seek? _____

39. According to 1 Thessalonians 2:4-5 does the preaching of the Gospel with flattering words do the hearers a **favor** or a **disservice**? Explain: _____
_____
_____

40. Read Galatians 1:11. Was the true Gospel being preached as a revelation from God or from man? _____

41. Read Galatians 1:12. How was Paul taught this Gospel? _____
_____

42. Read Galatians 1:12. How is it that you can receive this knowledge of the same Gospel?
_____

43. Read James 1:17-18. What comes down from the Father of lights?
_____

44. According to James 1:17, does God vary, or change? _____

45. Read James 1:18. How did God bring us forth? _____

46. Do you think God would treat you differently than Paul, a great man of God? _____

47. If Christ revealed Himself to Paul to preach the Gospel, does it stand to reason that He'd do the same for you? _____

48. Read Galatians 1:1-14. Why did Paul go into a short historical summary of his past zealousness? _____
_____
_____

49. Read Galatians 1:15-17. After Paul received a full revelation of Jesus Christ, what happened to all his traditions? _____

50. As you receive a greater revelation of Jesus Christ, what will happen to all of your traditions?
_____

51. Read Galatians 1:15. When did God call Paul?
    A. From his mother's womb.
    B. On the Damascus Road.

52. Read Galatians 1:16. What was God's plan for Paul?
_____

53. Read Acts 9:15. When Saul (Paul) was persecuting the Church, did God change His mind about His plans for him? _____

54. Read Romans 11:29. Do your past, present, or future behaviors alter, or change God's plan for your life? _____

55. Read Galatians 1:17. Did Paul seek the approval and acceptance of the apostles to establish his calling? _____

56. Since God's plan and calling upon your life are irrevocable, regardless of your past, are you still trying to gain man's approval for what God has called you to do? _____

57. Write out Proverbs 16:7.
_____
_____
_____

58. Read Galatians 1:20. Who was Paul accountable to for the words he spoke? _____

59. Who are you accountable to for the words you speak? _____

60. Read Acts 9:26-27. Why were the believers afraid to meet with Paul when he came to Jerusalem? _____

61. According to Acts 9:27, what happened to Paul and what did he do as a result?
_____

62. Read Galatians 1:23-24. What did the churches in Judea do after they had seen and heard Paul testify of Christ? _____

Galatians 1:1-24
Discipleship Answer Key

1. Read Galatians 1:1. What was Paul's purpose in emphasizing Who had called him to be a messenger for Jesus Christ?
   The false teachers were trying to discredit Paul's validity, not only the message of Christ, but his apostleship as well.

2. Read John 15:16. Did you choose Christ?
   No.

3. What two things did Christ do for you?
   1. He chose me.
   2. He appointed (ordained) me.

4. What was His purpose in choosing you?
   To go and bear fruit.

5. If you accept the calling of the Lord upon your life, what is the result of the fruit you bear?
   That it should remain.

6. Read John 15:16. What does the Lord promise you at the end of this verse?
   Whatever I ask the Father in His name, He will give me.

7. Read Acts 20:24. How did Paul view his life and purpose in life?
   Paul said that his life was worth nothing unless he spent it doing the work God had given him, which was sharing the Gospel of the grace of God and His wonderful love and kindness.

8. Read Romans 5:1-2 (AMP). **"Therefore, since we are justified (acquitted, declared righteous, and given a right standing with God) through faith, let us [grasp the fact that we] have [the peace of reconciliation to hold and to enjoy] peace with God through our Lord Jesus Christ (the Messiah, the Anointed One). 2) Through Him also we have [our] access (entrance, introduction) by faith into this grace (state of God's favor) in which we [firmly and safely] stand. And let us rejoice and exult in our hope of experiencing and enjoying the glory of God."**
   According to Romans 5:1, is your "justification by faith" something you earn and are still trying to attain?
   No, I am already justified.

9. What is the result of your justification?
   I have peace with God through Jesus Christ.

10. In verse Romans 5:2, what else do you have access to by your faith?
    God's grace.

11. What is your current posture in God's grace supposed to be according to this Scripture?
    A. **Firmly and safely standing**
    B. Faltering and barely hanging on
    C. Just missed it by a hair

12. Read Galatians 1:4. What was the purpose for Christ dying on the cross for our sins?
    To deliver us from this present evil world.

13. Read Galatians 1:4. Whose plan was it that Christ should die in your place?
    God's.

14. According to Galatians 1:4, can you be delivered, or rescued, from this "present evil world" by any other means?
    No.

15. According to the quote from the USB Handbook for Galatians 1:4, we have been given grace and peace "so that we do not have to live like people do in this present evil age." If you deny this grace and peace from God, you are essentially saying…
    A. Christ died in vain (Gal. 2:21).
    B. The Word of God is of no effect (Mark 7:13).
    C. **Both.**

16. Read Galatians 1:5. Who is to receive the glory for our justification and salvation?
    God the Father and Jesus Christ His Son.

17. Read Galatians 1:6. The error of the Galatians was not just a minor infraction. What was Paul "marveling" over?
    That they were being double-minded, turning to a false gospel, and deserting God Himself.

18. Read Galatians 1:6. What happens when you deny the grace of God that comes through Jesus Christ?
    You remove yourself from God.

19. Read Galatians 1:6. What were the people turning to and following?
    A different gospel.

20. Can you recognize any area of your own life where you have held on to the traditions of men while mixing it with the Gospel?
    Example: tithing, church attendance out of a sense of duty versus a true desire to worship.

21. If so, can you now see how any perversion of the true Gospel negates grace and peace?
    Yes

22. Read Galatians 1"7. Was the "new gospel" being preached merely a slight shading of the truth?
    No, it was completely different.

23. Read Acts 4:12. Is there any other way to heaven besides having faith in Jesus Christ?
No.

24. Are there still people today who are deceived and pervert the truth causing confusion among those seeking to follow Christ?
Yes.
Can you name an example?
Some denominational religions and cults.

25. Read Galatians 1:8. Is preaching a twisted gospel a serious violation of the truth?
Very serious, bringing condemnation and a curse.

26. Read Galatians 1:8. Is anyone on earth or in heaven exempt from this potential curse?
No.

27. Read Galatians 1:3. What was the Gospel that had already preached?
Grace and peace through Christ.

28. Have you ever been so emphatic about something that you repeated yourself several times?
Yes.

29. What was your purpose in doing so?
So the hearer wouldn't forget what I was saying.

30. Read Galatians 1:9. How important did Paul feel it was to not distort the Gospel?
Extremely important.

31. Read Galatians 1:10. Was Paul out to win a popularity contest?
No.

32. According to Galatians 1:10, what was Paul's primary motivation, regardless the cost, in rebuking these Christians?
He was motivated by his love for Jesus and his desire to serve Him.

33. What is your motive in sharing the Gospel?

34. Read 2 Timothy 4:2-4. What is the first charge given here?
Preach the word.

35. According to 2 Timothy 4:2, what three things are we also instructed to do when preaching the Word of God?
   1. **Reprove**
   2. **rebuke**
   3. **exhort**

36. Read 2 Timothy 4:2. How is the Word of God to be delivered?
With longsuffering (patience) and doctrine (teaching).

37. Regardless if you always speak the truth, will all men always agree with you?
No.

38. Read 1 Thessalonians 2:4-6. When Paul preached the Gospel, whose approval did he seek?
He wanted to please God.

39. According to 1 Thessalonians 2:4-5 does the preaching of the Gospel with flattering words do the hearers a **favor** or a **disservice**?
Disservice.
Explain: **The gospel is to convince, rebuke, and exhort others in the way of the Lord. If any other gospel is preached, God is not given the opportunity to rescue the perishing from hell.**

40. Read Galatians 1:11. Was the true Gospel being preached a revelation from God or from man?
As a revelation from God.

41. Read Galatians 1:12. How was Paul taught this Gospel?
Thru the revelation of Jesus Christ.

42. Read Galatians 1:12. How is it that you can receive this knowledge of the same Gospel?
Thru the revelation of Jesus Christ.

43. Read James 1:17-18. What comes down from the Father of lights?
Every good and perfect gift.

44. According to James 1:18, does God vary, or change?
No.

45. Read James 1:18. How did God bring us forth?
By the word of truth.

46. Do you think God would treat you differently than Paul, a great man of God?
No.

47. If Christ revealed Himself to Paul to preach the Gospel, does it stand to reason that He'd do the same for you?
Yes.

48. Read Galatians 1:13-14. Why did Paul go into a short historical summary of his past zealousness?
To again establish the fact that his religious zealousness was not based upon the revelation of Christ, but rather the traditions of man.

49. Read Galatians 1:15-17. After Paul received a full revelation of Jesus Christ, what happened to all his traditions?
Paul left them behind and followed Christ.

50. As you receive a greater revelation of Jesus Christ, what will happen to all of your traditions?

51. Read Galatians 1:15. When did God call Paul?
    A. From his mother's womb.
    B. On the Damascus Road.

52. Read Galatians 1:16. What was God's plan for Paul?
To preach among the heathen.

53. Read Acts 9:15. When Saul (Paul) was persecuting the Church, did God change His mind about His plans for him?
No.

54. Read Romans 11:29. Do your past, present, or future behaviors alter, or change, God's plan for your life?
No, the gifts and calling of God are irrevocable.

55. Read Galatians 1:17. Did Paul seek the approval and acceptance of the apostles to establish his calling?
No.

56. Since God's plan and calling upon your life are irrevocable, regardless of your past, are you still trying to gain man's approval for what God has called you to do?
When a man's ways please the Lord, He makes even his enemies be at peace with him.

57. Write out Proverbs 16:7.
_____
_____
_____

58. Read Galatians 1:20. Who was Paul accountable to for the words he spoke?
God.

59. Who are you accountable to for the words you speak?
God.

60. Read Acts 9:26-27. Why were the believers afraid to meet with Paul when he came to Jerusalem?
They were afraid of him and didn't believe he was really a disciple.

61. According to Acts 9:27, what happened to Paul and what did he do as a result?
Paul saw the Lord on the road to Damascus, and he was boldly preaching in the name of the Lord.

62. Read Galatians 1:23-24. What did the churches in Judea do after they had seen and heard Paul testify of Christ?
They gave glory to God.

Galatians 2:1-21
Discipleship Commentary

....

Galatians 2:1

Then fourteen years after I went up again to Jerusalem with Barnabas, and took Titus with me also. (KJV)

Fourteen years later I went back to Jerusalem with Barnabas, taking Titus along with me. (TEV)

(Gal. 2:1-10) There are two things in this section of Scripture that would verify the validity of Paul's message of salvation by grace: (1) Titus, who was a Greek, was not compelled to be circumcised (Gal. 2:3), proving that salvation was through faith without the works of the law (Gal. 2:16). (2) Paul's Gospel of grace was approved by the leaders of the "mother church," the church of Jerusalem (Gal. 2:6-9).

(Gal. 2:1) The book of Acts records five visits that Paul made to Jerusalem: "(1) The visit after Paul left Damascus (Acts 9:26-30, Gal. 1:18-20). (2) The famine visit (Acts 11:27-30). (3) The visit to attend the Jerusalem Council (Acts 15:1-30). (4) The visit at the end of the second missionary journey (Acts 18:22). (5) The final visit, which resulted in Paul's imprisonment and trial (Acts 21:15 – 23:25)" (TBKC, p. 593).

This second visit to Jerusalem, which was 14 years after Paul's first one, is thought to be the famine relief visit, the council of Jerusalem visit, or possibly neither one, for Paul was directed to go up by revelation at this time. There is a diversity of opinion about this.

"If this second visit is indeed the Council of Jerusalem visit, it appears that 'after Paul's arrival in Jerusalem there was first a private conference with the elders of the church (Gal. 2:1-9), and then the conference representing the entire church which Luke describes.'" (TETG, p. 47 [Acts 15:1-29])

Paul's companions on this visit were Barnabas, a Jewish brother that helped evangelize and establish the Galatian churches on Paul's first missionary journey (Acts 13-14), and Titus, a Gentile convert to Christ, but not submitted to the Jewish rites of circumcision.

Galatians 2:2

And I went up by revelation, and communicated unto them that gospel which I preach among the Gentiles, but privately to them, which were of reputation, lest by any means I should run, or had run, in vain. (KJV)

But I went there because God had told me to go, and I explained the good news that I had been preaching to the Gentiles. Then I met privately with the ones who seemed to be the most important leaders. I wanted to make sure that all my work in the past and my future work would not be for nothing. (CEV)

I went there with definite orders from God to confer with the brothers there about the message I was preaching to the Gentiles. I talked privately to the leaders of the church so that they would all understand just what I had been teaching and, I hoped, agree that it was right. (LB)

I went up because God showed me that I should go. I went to those men who were the leaders. When we were alone, I explained to them about the gospel which I preached to non-Jewish people, so that my past work and the work I do now would not be wasted. (SE)

I went to clarify with them what had been revealed to me. At that time I placed before them exactly what I was preaching to the non-Jews. I did this in private with the leaders, those held in esteem by the church, so that our concern would not become a controversial public issue, marred by ethnic tension, exposing my years of work to denigration and endangering my present ministry. (TM)

(Gal. 2:2) This verse states the reason Paul's visit is by a "revelation." It has now been 14 years since Paul has been to Jerusalem. Paul, among the Gentiles, had done much preaching work. It has been revealed by God to Paul that it is time to communicate, to lie out, (Greek. – to set forth in words) the Gospel that he has been preaching to the Jerusalem church. If Jerusalem is preaching a different Gospel, Paul's work could be stopped, and his work would be in vain. He laid the Gospel out first "unto them" (the Jerusalem church, and then privately, in a deeper and more systematic way, to them which were of reputation, i.e., men of recognized position, the church leaders. Three such leaders were mentioned (Gal. 2:9) – James the Lord's brother and overseer of the Jerusalem church, John the apostle and son of Zebedee, and the Apostle Peter who had already been called before the Jerusalem church for his work among the Gentiles (Acts 11:1-18).

So the "big four" are together—Peter, James, John, and Paul—to discuss the problem of the Gospel and the Law among the Jews and Gentiles.

The Judaizers are assuming that the leaders of the church will take their side against Paul and his Gospel (Acts 15:1-2).

Galatians 2:3

But neither Titus, who was with me, being a Greek, was compelled to be circumcised: (KJV)

But [all went well]: even Titus, who was with me, was not compelled [as some had anticipated] to be circumcised although he was a Greek. (AMP)

Significantly, Titus, non-Jewish though he was, was not required to be circumcised. (TM)

(Gal. 2:3) Paul had brought Titus on this trip as a test case of a full-fledged, converted Gentile to faith in Jesus Christ. If Titus were forced to be circumcised, the truth of the Gospel would be compromised.

The apostles received Titus, and the truth remained that man is justified by faith in Jesus Christ and not by the works of the Law (Gal. 2:16).

Galatians 2:4

And that because of false brethren unawares brought in, who came in privily to spy out our liberty which we have in Christ Jesus, that they might bring us into bondage: (KJV)

Pretending to be fellow believers, these men slipped into our group as spies, in order to find out about the freedom we have through our union with Christ Jesus. They wanted to make slaves of us, (TEV)

Even that question wouldn't have come up except for some so-called "Christians" there – false ones, really – who came to spy on us and see what freedom we enjoyed in Christ, Jesus, as to whether we obeyed the Jewish laws or not. They tried to get us all tied up in their rules, like slaves in chains. (LB)

Some men who called themselves Christians asked about this. They got into our meeting without being asked. They came there to find out how free we are who belong to Christ. They tried to get us to be chained to the Jewish law. (TNLT)

While we were in conference we were infiltrated by spies pretending to be Christians, who slipped in to find out just how free true Christians are. Their ulterior motive was to reduce us to their brand of servitude. (TM)

(Gal. 2:4) This matter of justification by Law plus faith in Christ arose, because false brethren had infiltrated the church, spying on spiritual liberty in Christ and wishing to bring believers into religious bondage (Acts 15:1-2). These legalists had already infiltrated the ranks of true Christianity as described in similar scriptures such as Jude 3-4 (a perversion of grace) and 1 Timothy 1:7 (a perversion of the Law).

Paul speaks of these religious people, who wanted to mix faith in Christ and Jewish circumcision for justification, as "false brethren." Paul is later going to state, "if you are counting on circumcision and keeping the Jewish laws to make you right with God, then Christ cannot save you." (Gal. 5:2, LB)

This shows us that claiming to be Christians and yet embracing a false gospel will bring one into a state of false Christianity.

Galatians 2:5

To whom we gave place by subjection, no, not for an hour; that the truth of the gospel might continue with you. (KJV)

But we refused to yield for a single instant to their claims; we were determined that the truth of the gospel should hold good for you. (MOF)

But we did not listen to them for a single moment, for we did not want to confuse you into thinking that salvation can be earned by being circumcised and by obeying Jewish laws. (LB)

We didn't give them the time of day. We were determined to preserve the truth of the Message for you. (TM)

(Gal. 2:5) The real question of Galatians 2:5 is, "Will the truth of the Gospel remain?" It is clear from this little epistle that a person may begin with a true dependence upon Christ and Him crucified for total acceptance before God and then return to the Law mentality of self-effort for acceptance. As Paul says, "Will the truth of the Gospel continue with you?"

Paul would not submit himself for a moment to the mixture of the Law and grace lest the Gospel of Christ be perverted.

Galatians 2:6

But of these who seemed to be somewhat, (whatsoever they were, it maketh no matter to me; God accepteth no man's person:) for they who seemed to be somewhat in conference added nothing to me: (KJV)

As for those who seemed to be important – whatever they were makes no difference to me; God does not judge by external appearance – those men added nothing to my message. (NIV)

As for those who were considered important in the church, their reputation doesn't concern me. God isn't impressed with mere appearances, and neither am I. And the leaders were able to add nothing to the message I had been preaching. (TM)

(Gal. 2:6) The perversion of the original Gospel was not that something was taken away from it but rather that something was added to it. When Paul presented his Gospel to the apostles, they added nothing to it. In other words, it was complete as preached by Paul. Nothing more was added to it or taken from it.

Galatians 2:7-9

But contrariwise, when they say that the gospel of the uncircumcision was committed unto me, as the gospel of the circumcision was unto Peter; (For he that wrought effectually in Peter to the apostleship of the circumcision, the same was mighty in me toward the Gentiles;) And when James, Cephas, and John, who seemed to be pillars, perceived the grace that was given unto me, they gave me and Barnabas the right hands of fellowship; that we should go unto the heathen, and they unto the circumcision. (KJV)

In fact, when Peter, James and John, who were known as the pillars of the church, saw how greatly God has used me in winning the Gentiles, just as Peter had been blessed so greatly in his preaching to the Jews- for the same God gave us each our special gifts, - they shook hands with Barnabas and me and encouraged us to keep right on with our preaching to the Gentiles while they continued their work with the Jews. (LB)

I was soon evident that God had entrusted me with the same message to the non-Jews and Peter had been preaching to the Jews. Recognizing that my calling had been given by God, James, Peter and John – the pillars of the church – shook hands with me and Barnabas, assigning us to a ministry to the non-Jews, while they continued to be responsible for reaching out to the Jews. (TM)

(Gal. 2:7-9) There were not two different gospels preached by Peter and Paul – a gospel of the circumcision and a gospel of the uncircumcision. For there is only one true Gospel, as stated by Paul earlier in Galatians 1:6-7.

The phrase "for he that wrought effectually" carries the idea that God was using Peter in a mighty way among the Jews, and God was using Paul in a mighty way among the Gentiles.

The term "the right hands of fellowship" implies a united missionary effort and partnership to work together for the spreading of the Gospel among Jews and Gentiles, especially Peter with Jews and Paul with the Gentiles.

The "grace" that was given to Paul and perceived by the pillars of the church – James, Cephas, and John – was the effective working of God's power that was demonstrated through the ministry of Paul to the Gentiles. Paul spoke many times about God's ability working through him and not any ability of his own (Eph. 3:1-3, 7; 1 Cor. 15:9-10).

Galatians 2:10

Only they would that we should remember the poor; the same which I also was forward to do. (KJV)

They asked us to do only one thing – to remember the needy in their group, which is the very thing I have been eager to do. (SE)

All they asked was that we should remember the needy in their group, which is the very thing I have been eager to do. (TEV)

(Gal. 2:10) This agreement that Paul and Barnabas would continue work among the Gentiles, while Peter, James, and John were to concentrate upon Jews, ended with a final request and agreement that Paul should remember the poor. In the Greek, the tense and the verb carry the idea "the we should keep on remembering the poor" (*Wuest Word Studies in Greek, Volume I*, p. 68). The Today's English Version implies that the "poor" being spoken of here were the needy saints of Jerusalem and Judea. "All they asked was that we should remember the needy in their group, which is the very thing I have been eager to do." Paul had already done this on a previous occasion (Acts 11:27-30) and would continue to do so in his future missionary journeys (1 Cor. 16:1-3, Rom. 15:26-27).

Galatians 2:11-12

But when Peter was come to Antioch, I withstood him to the face, because he was to be blamed. For before that certain came from James, he did eat with the Gentiles: but when they were come, he withdrew and separated himself, fearing them which were of the circumcision. (KJV)

But when Peter came to Antioch I had to oppose him publicly, speaking strongly against what he was doing, for it was very wrong. For when he first arrived he ate with the Gentile Christians [who don't bother with circumcision and the many Jewish laws]. But afterwards when some Jewish friends of James came, he wouldn't eat with the Gentiles anymore because he was afraid of what these Jewish legalists, who insisted that circumcision was necessary for salvation, would say. (LB)

Later, when Peter came to Antioch, I had a face-to-face confrontation with him because he was clearly out of line. Here's the situation. Earlier, before certain persons had come from James, Peter regularly ate with the non-Jews. But when that conservative group came from Jerusalem, he cautiously pulled back and put as much distance as he could manage between himself and his non-Jewish friends. That's how fearful he was of the conservative Jewish clique that's been pushing the old system of circumcision. (TM)

(Gal.2:11-12) A certain aspect of the Gospel had been revealed to Peter by divine revelation from the Lord just as the Gospel was revealed to Paul. This aspect of revelation dealt with Peter's vision about dietary laws of Leviticus 11, Deuteronomy 14, and its relation to the Gentiles' acceptance into the body of Christ. Even though it was unlawful for a Jew to associate with or visit a Gentile (Acts 10:28), the Lord Jesus showed Peter the cleansing of foods and the acceptance of all men through the Gospel (Acts 10:28, 34-38).

Now Peter is visiting the church at Antioch, a predominantly Gentile church, but it did contain some Jews (Gal 2:13). As Peter was enjoying his acceptance with God through the Lord Jesus Christ, he was free to enjoy his Christian liberty. He ate with the Gentiles, partook in their Christian love feasts, and possibly ate foods that were considered unclean by the Mosaic Law. At just that time, some Jewish brethren from Jerusalem arrived at Antioch. Because of religious fear that some legalists might see him break tradition, he withdrew from eating with the Gentiles and became a hypocrite. Because this action was more than just Christian liberty, but in fact an action that projected that Jew and Gentile were not "one new man" through faith in Christ Jesus, Paul opposed and rebuked Peter publicly in front of the whole church.

Galatians 2:13

And the other Jews dissembled likewise with him; insomuch that Barnabas also was carried away with their dissimulation. (KJV)

The other Jews joined him in his hypocrisy, so that by their hypocrisy even Barnabas was led astray. (NIV)

He and the other Jews hid their true feelings so well that even Barnabas was fooled. (CEV)

The rest of the Jewish Christians, too, joined him in this pretense, so that even Barnabas was influenced to join them in their pretense. (Wms)

Peter was two-faced. The other Jewish believers joined Peter. They were two-faced, too. Even Barnabas was influenced by the things which those Jewish believers did. (SE)

Unfortunately, the rest of the Jews in the Antioch church joined in that hypocrisy so that even Barnabas was swept along in the charade. (TM)

(Gal. 2:13) The pressure was on. Obviously, these Jewish believers from James felt that the Law that divided the Jews from the Gentiles was still in effect. Peter's action, not his belief, was an influence that also caused the other Jewish believers in Antioch to follow Peter's hypocrisy. Although Peter and the others certainly knew better, their actions compromised the Gospel and, in effect, reconstructed the middle wall of partition (Eph. 2:14-15). Even Barnabas, a great companion of Paul and minister to the Gentiles, was led astray by Peter's example. Although Barnabas came from Cyprus (a Gentile center), he was also associated with the Jerusalem church and was their delegate to Antioch (Acts 4:36-37, 9:26-30, and 11:22-26). This also could have been such a great pressure to Barnabas that he felt he had to pacify and please these Jerusalem brethren.

Galatians 2:14

But when I saw that they walked not uprightly according to the truth of the gospel, I said unto Peter before them all, If thou, being a Jew, livest after the manner of Gentiles, and not as do the Jews, why compellest thou the Gentiles to live as do the Jews? (KJV)

But when I saw that this behaviour was a contradiction of the truth of the gospel, I said to Cephas so that everyone could hear, "If you, who are a Jew, do not live like a Jew but like a Gentile, why do you try to make Gentiles live like Jews?" (J.B. Phil)

But when I saw that they were not straightforward about the truth of the gospel, I said to Cephas before them all, "If you, though a Jew, live like a Gentile and not like a Jew, how can you compel the Gentiles to live like Jews?" (RSV)

But when I saw that they were not maintaining a steady, straight course according to the Message, I spoke up to Peter in front of them all: "If you, a Jew, live like a non-Jew when you're not being observed by the watchdogs from Jerusalem, what right do you have to require non-Jews to conform to Jewish customs just to make a favorable impression on your old Jerusalem cronies?" (TM)

(Gal. 2:14) When Paul saw that Peter and the rest of the Jews' conduct did not follow the true path of the Gospel, he said to Peter before the whole Christian congregation at Antioch, "If you, though a Jew, live like the Gentiles and not like the Jews, you have no right to make the Gentiles copy Jewish ways" (JB).

"By drawing back Peter was actually forcing the Gentile Christians to find ways to be acceptable to the Jewish Christians, and that way could very well be by following the Jewish law, which in effect would make them live like Jews" (*USB Handbook*, p. 43). Peter, by his conduct, was denying the truth that the Gospel proclaims, "In Christ Jesus neither circumcision availeth anything, nor uncircumcision, but a new creature" (Gal. 6:15)

Galatians 2:15-16

We who are Jews by nature, and not sinners of the Gentiles, knowing that a man is not justified by the works of the law, but by faith of Jesus Christ, even we have believed in Jesus Christ, that we might be justified by the faith of Christ, and not by the works of the law: for by the works of the law shall no flesh be justified. (KJV)

Indeed, we are Jews by birth and not "Gentile sinners," as they are called. Yet we know that a person is put right with God only through faith in Jesus Christ, never by doing what the Law requires. We, too, have believed in Christ in order to be put right with God through our faith in Christ, and not by doing what the Law requires. (TEV)

We Jews know that we have no advantage of birth over "non-Jewish sinners." We know very well that we are not set right with God by rule keeping but only through personal faith in Jesus Christ. How do we know? We tried it – and we had the best system of rules the world has ever seen! Convinced that no human being can please God by self-improvement, we believed in Jesus as the Messiah so that we might be set right before God by trusting in the Messiah, not by trying to be good." (TM)

(Gal. 2:15-16) Paul is now stating to Peter, "We who are Jews by birth and not 'Gentile sinners,' know that a man is not declared righteous by the works of the law but by faith in Christ" (TEV, KJV).

Paul is using a term used by Pharisaic Jews that describes all people outside the covenant of the Law as being "Gentile sinners." Paul goes on to say that "no man is declared righteous by the works of the Law but by the faith of (in) Jesus Christ." Although the Law of Moses is being spoken of here, this can also be understood as any religious law (what day you worship, the length of hair you should have, your clothes, the mode of baptism, or other religious codes), for those works can justify no person.

The term "works of the law" is used seven times in the New Testament in five scriptures (Rom. 9:32; Gal. 2:16; 3:2, 5, and 10).

What are "works of the law"? Any rule, command, or law that a person observes in an attempt to meet God's standard of righteousness for acceptance and right-standing before God. In other words, a righteousness produced by one's self, a righteousness belonging to one's self, offered to God as a means of meeting God's standard for acceptance. Philippians 3:9 says it's "having MINE OWN RIGHTEOUSNESS [a righteousness belonging to me] which is of the law." (Read Romans 9:30 – Romans 10:10 for a fuller understanding of the "works of the law").

"Works of the law" have always been man, as well as the religious systems of the world's attempt to be accepted by God. Paul says, Let me "be found in Him [Christ] not having a righteousness of my own that comes from the law, but that which is through faith in Christ—the righteousness that comes from God and is by faith" (Phil. 3:9, NIV).

It takes a radical revelation of the Gospel of grace to abandon faith in the works of the Law. For men have not realized that God's standard of righteousness is the RIGHTEOUSNESS OF GOD alone.

Charles Swindoll in his book *The Grace Awakening* states, "Justification is the sovereign act of God whereby He declares righteous the believing sinner—while he is still in a sinning state" (p.24).

Donald Barnhouse stated, "God…credits…this man Abraham to be perfect even at a moment when Abraham was ungodly in himself. That is justification" (Rom. Vol. 3, p. 208

[Rom. 4:5]).

This is the first time the term "justified" is used in this epistle. It means: (1) To "justify" meaning "to declare righteous," not "to make righteous." It is the opposite of condemnation (Rom. 8:33-34). (2) It is a word used in reference to trial and judgment—a word that belongs to the law court (Deut. 25:1). It is in every sense a verdict of the judge. It means to be declared righteous by divine sentence; acquitted in the judgment of God, judged righteous at God's tribunal" (*Justification*, Robert Brinsmead, p. 58). (3) Being a legal word, it is related to the law. To 'justify' means, "setting one right before law" (*Systematic Theology*, Augustus Strong, p. 856). "Sanctification, i.e. faith working by love is the fruit of justification. The Christian life and experience are not the gospel but the fruit of the gospel" (*Justification*, R. Brinsmead, p. 64).

Galatians 2:17-18

But if, while we seek to be justified by Christ, we ourselves also are found sinners, is therefore Christ the minister of sin? God forbid. For if I build again the things which I destroyed, I make myself a transgressor. (KJV)

But what if we trust Christ to save us and then find that we are wrong, and that we cannot be saved without being circumcised and obeying all the other Jewish laws? Wouldn't we need to say that faith in Christ had ruined us? God forbid that anyone should dare to think such things about our Lord. Rather, we are sinners if we start rebuilding the old system I have been destroying, of trying to be saved by keeping Jewish laws. (LB)

If, then, as we try to be put right with God by our union with Christ, we are found to be sinners as much as the Gentiles are – does this mean that Christ is serving the cause of sin? By no means! If I start to rebuild the system of Law that I tore down, then I show myself to be someone who breaks the Law. (TEV)

Have some of you noticed that we are not yet perfect? (No great surprise, right?) And are you ready to make the accusation that since people like me, who go through Christ in order to get things right with God, aren't perfectly virtuous, Christ must therefore be an accessory to sin? The accusation is frivolous. If I was "trying to be good," I would be rebuilding the same old barn that I tore down. I would be

acting as a charlatan. (TM)

(Gal. 2:17-18) Verse 17 is a very difficult scripture to interpret, but it seems that Paul is saying, "If I am seeking justification in Christ alone, then it requires that I abandon self-righteousness (faith in keeping the Law as a means of attaining righteousness). If it is wrong that Christ alone can save and I'm found to be a sinner, then Christ is the one that promoted or furthered that sin (because I abandoned the Law so that I could trust Him alone)."

Rather than that being the case, Paul says, "If I build up the old system of obeying the Law (works of righteousness) to be saved, in reality, I've only made myself a transgressor, i.e., a lawbreaker." For the Law is a complete system that must be obeyed in it's entirety (James 2:10-11), or it brings one under a curse (Gal. 3:10). It never brought one into salvation, for its power is in the strength of the flesh (to keep all the dos and resist all the don'ts). It was destined to failure as a means of salvation because: (1) It was a complete unit that must not be broken in any area. (2) It would fail because of the weakness of our sinful flesh (Rom. 8:3).

Galatians 2:19

For I through the law am dead to the law, that I might live unto God. (KJV)

For under the Law I "died" and now I am dead to the Law's demands so that I may live for God. (J.B. Phil.)

What actually took place is this: I tried keeping rules and working my head off to please God and it didn't work. So I quit being a "law man" so that I could be "God's man." (TM)

(Gal. 2:19) It was through the Law that I was released form the Law. The law said, "live perfectly or you must die." "The soul that sinneth, it shall die" (Ezek. 18:4, 20). I sinned and I died. But when did I die? I was crucified with Christ (v. 20). When He died, I died. He died to satisfy a broken Law. After death, there is no more that the Law could do to me. Through death I've been released from the control or domination of the Law. The just demands of the Law have been met, satisfied, and released from me by the death of Jesus Christ. Now I am free to live in a total relationship with God. This relationship is totally by grace through faith (Romans 5:1-2, 7:4, 9).

Galatians 2:20

I am crucified with Christ: nevertheless I live; yet not I, but Christ liveth in me: and the life which I now live in the flesh I live by the faith of the Son of God, who loved me, and gave Himself for me. (KJV)

I have been crucified with Chris; and I live now not with my own life but with the life of Christ who lives in me. The life I now live in this body I live in faith: faith in the Son of God who loved me and who sacrificed Himself for my sake. (TJB)

Christ's life showed me how, and enabled me to do it. I identified myself completely with Him. Indeed, I have been crucified with Christ. Me ego is no longer central. It is no longer important that I appear righteous before you or have your good opinion, and I am no longer driven to impress God. Christ lives in me. The life you see me living is not "mine," but it is lived by faith in the Son of God, who loved me and gave Himself for me. I am not going to go back on that. (TM)

(Gal. 2:20) Verse 20 is connected to verse 19 by declaring the believer's death to the Law by being crucified with Christ. Paul is saying, "Under the old system of the law, the 'I' was prominent, it was the 'I' that lived. To depend on the law is to put emphasis on ONE'S OWN POWERS to do what it requires" (*USB Handbook*, p. 50).

Paul is stating that the way that I live now is through dependence upon Christ who loved me and gave Himself for me. This faith is built on the fact of Christ's personal love for us.

Galatians 2:21

I do not frustrate the grace of God: for if righteousness come by the law, then Christ is dead in vain. (KJV)

This gift is from God, and it is very important to me. Because if the law could have made us right with God, then Christ died for nothing! (SE)

I say that we are not to put aside the loving favor of God. If we could be made right with God by keeping the Jewish law, then Christ died for nothing. (TNLT)

Is it not clear to you that to go back to that old rule-keeping, peer-pleasing religion would be an abandonment of everything personal and free in my relationship with God? I refuse to do that, to repudiate God's grace. If a living relationship with God could come by rule keeping, then Christ died unnecessarily. (TM)

(Gal. 2:21) "The word 'frustrate' suggests defeating in the sense of nullifying another's accomplishment or making it ineffective" (AH Dict.). If righteousness, i.e., salvation, could come through obedience to Law, then Christ's accomplishments on the cross have been nullified, defeated, and made ineffective.

Paul is stating (this is how the Greek word is used), "I'm not despising, rejecting, bringing to nothing, frustrating, disannulling, or casting off God's grace by seeking justification through the Law."

Galatians 2:1-21
Discipleship Questions

1. Read Acts 4:36. According to the Discipleship Commentary for Galatians 2:1, who was Barnabas? _____

2. Read Galatians 2:3. According to the Discipleship Commentary of Galatians 2:1, who was Titus? _____

3. Read Galatians 2:2. What message did Paul deliver to the Jerusalem church? _____

4. Read Galatians 1:15-16 and Acts 9:15. How did Paul receive this message he preached among the Gentiles? _____

5. Read Galatians 2:2. Paul was a man of authority. How did he treat those who were of authority in Jerusalem? _____

6. Read Galatians 2:2 in The Message Bible. Name three reasons Paul met with Peter, James, and John privately.
    A. _____
    B. _____
    C. _____

7. Read Galatians 1:16-17. Do you think Paul was seeking their approval to validate his ministry? _____ Explain: _____

8. Read Galatians 1:18, and combining it with Galatians 2:1 how many years had Paul been in the ministry? _____

9. Read Galatians 2:2. What did Paul say his work and ministry efforts were if the Jerusalem elders disagreed with the Gospel he was preaching? _____

10. Read Galatians 2:3. Was Titus required to follow the customary Jewish laws and be circumcised? _____

11. Read Galatians 2:4. How was it known that Titus wasn't circumcised? _____

12. Read Acts 15:1. What did the legalistic Jews believe the Gentiles must do in order to be saved? _____

13. Read Galatians 2:4. If the deceptive plan that the legalistic Jews had of spying on the liberty of Paul and his co-workers had worked, what message would that have sent to the people regarding the Gospel that Paul was preaching? _____

14. Read Galatians 1:8-9. What is to become of these "false-Christians" who teach that what Jesus did for us in order to be accepted by God was not enough?

15. _____

    Read Galatians 2:5. Write out the noted translations regarding Paul's reactions to this covert manipulation.
    A. Moffat - _____
    B. Living Bible - _____
16. C. The Message - _____

    Read Galatians 2:5 in the Living Bible. Why wouldn't Paul budge, even just a little?

17. _____

    Read Galatians 2:5 in the Message Bible. What was their reaction to this religious manipulation? _____
18. _____

    Read Hosea 4:6 and Ephesians 4:14. What causes people to be carried away by every wind of doctrine? _____
19. _____

    Read Ephesians 4:11-12. Why were the gifts of the apostles, prophets, evangelists, pastors, and teachers given to the church?
    A. _____
20. B. _____

    Read Ephesians 4:13-15. What is the result of this equipping and edifying?
    A. _____
    B. _____
    C. _____
21. D. _____

    Read Ephesians 4:14. What is a person considered if he or she is still swayed by the "doctrines of man"?
22. _____

    Read Ephesians 4:4. What is the result of knowing the truth? _____
23. _____

24. Read Galatians 2:6. Was Paul impressed with manly titles or lofty positions? _____

25. When dealing with people, what is the most important thing to consider:
   A. Position and Reputation
   B. Godly Character

26. Read Acts 2:11. Does God treat everyone the same? _____

27. Read Proverbs 16:2 in the Amplified Bible "All the ways of man are pure in his own eyes, but the Lord weighs the spirits (thoughts and intents of the heart.)" What does the Lord weigh?

28. Is it possible to have a good idea, but a wrong motive? _____

29. Read Acts 15:11. What was the "Gospel for the uncircumcised"? _____

30. Read Romans 3:28. What was the "Gospel for the circumcised"? _____

31. Read Galatians 2:7-9. As Paul privately and systematically discussed to those of reputation the Gospel he was preaching to the Gentiles (2:2), what did those in the meeting perceive about Paul? _____

32. Read Galatians 2:9. Once Peter, James, and John realized Paul and Barnabas were all part of the same team, playing by the same rules, what was their reaction? _____

33. Read Ephesians 4:1-6. What are the five ways stated to walk worthy of your calling?
   A. _____
   B. _____
   C. _____
   D. _____
   E. _____

34. Read 1 Corinthians 1:10. What was Paul pleading to the Corinthians?
   A. _____
   B. _____
   C. _____
   D. _____

35. Read Galatians 2:10. What was Peter's only desire, or request, of Paul? _____

36. Read James 2:1-9. Is it pleasing to the Lord if a Christian who claims to have faith in Jesus

shows respect or favors to some people more than others?
37. _____

Read James 2:8. How is the royal law fulfilled according to this Scripture?
38. _____

Read Galatians 2:11-12. Why did Paul confront Peter?
39. _____
_____

40. Read Galatians 2:11. Why did Paul feel it was necessary to confront him? _____

41. _____
Read Galatians 2:4. What was Peter experiencing with the Gentiles before the "religious" Judaizers came to town? _____
42.
Read Galatians 2:12. What compelled Peter to hypocrisy? _____

Read Galatians 2:13. What was the consequence of Peter's hypocrisy? _____
43. _____

Read Galatians 2:13. Why did Paul make it a point to mention that even Barnabas got
44. carried away with their hypocrisy?
_____

45. If you sway from the truth even a little, what effect can it have on those around you?
_____

Read Galatians 2:5. What was Paul's response to the pressure of man-pleasing Judaizers?
_____

46. Read Galatians 2:14. What was Paul's concern regarding their hypocrisy, which was revealed by their actions?
    A. He was mad because he wasn't invited.
47. B. The motive behind their actions wasn't right.
    C. He and Barnabas already had dinner plans.

48. Read Galatians 1:8-9. What is Paul's stand in regards to presenting the "true gospel"?

49. _____
Read Titus 1:10-11. What were the Judaizers' motive behind their idle talk, deception, and
50. distorted teachings? _____

51. Read Titus 1:16. What happens when a person talks the talk but doesn't walk the walk?
_____

Complete the cliché. "_____ what you preach."
52.

53. Read Philippians 3:4-5. Was Paul a real Jew? _____

54. Read Galatians 2:16. What must every individual do in order to be justified before God? _____

55. Read Romans 3:20. Can anyone be made right by doing what the Law demands? _____

56. Read Romans 8:23-28. How are we made right with God? _____

57. Read Galatians 2:16. If you are "declared righteous" by the faith of Jesus Christ, how do you make yourself a transgressor or Law breaker? _____

58. Read Romans 8:3. Can we ever keep the Law to be righteous? _____

59. Read James 2:10-11. Is the Law a complete system that must be kept and obeyed in its entirety? _____

60. Read Galatians 2:17-18. Does Christ promote sin by releasing us from bondage to a legalistic system? _____

61. Read 2 Corinthians 3:5. Is your sufficiency from **YOURSELF** or **GOD** ?

62. Read 2 Corinthians 3:6. What has a believer been qualified for and made a minister

63. of? _____

64. Read 2 Corinthians 3:6. What does the "letter," or Law, do? _____

Read 2 Corinthians 3:6. What does the Spirit give? _____

65. Read Hebrews 8:7. Was the first covenant faultless? _____

Was the Old Covenant of the Law meant to survive?

66. _____

Read Galatians 2:19. According to this verse, what happened to you through the Law?

67. _____

Read Romans 7:4. If you were crucified with Christ, can the Law any longer have power over you? _____

68. Read Galatians 2:20. What does this verse say has happened to you through Christ? _____

Read Galatians 2:20. The crucifixion and resurrection of Jesus brings us new life. According to this verse, who lives in us, and how are we able to now live this life? _____

69. _____

Read Galatians 2:20 in The Message Bible. What four things happen when you are crucified with Christ?

70.   A._____
      B._____
71.   C._____
      D._____

Read Galatians 2:21. What happens when you treat God's gift of grace as something of minor importance, setting it aside and invalidating it?

_____

Read Galatians 3:21. Can the Law make us right with God? _____

72.

Read Romans 5:17. When we receive God's abundant grace and the gift of righteousness, we will:

73.   A. Declare that Christ did not die in vain.
      B. Reign in life by Jesus Christ.
      C. Have a living and vital relationship with God.
      D. All of the above

Read 1 Corinthians 1:18. What is the message of the cross to those who are perishing?

_____

What is the message of the cross to those who are being saved?

_____

Galatians 2:1-21
Discipleship Answer Key

1. Read Acts 4:36. According to the Discipleship Commentary for Galatians 2:1, who was Barnabas?
   A Jewish brother who helped evangelize and establish the Galatian churches.

2. Read Galatians 2:3. According to the Discipleship Commentary of Galatians 2:1, who was Titus?
   A Gentile convert.

3. Read Galatians 2:2. What message did Paul deliver to the Jerusalem church?
   He told them the Gospel he was preaching among the Gentiles.

4. Read Galatians 1:15-16 and Acts 9:15. How did Paul receive this message he preached among the Gentiles?
   By revelation from Jesus Christ.

5. Read Galatians 2:2. Paul was a man of authority. How did he treat those who were of authority in Jerusalem?
   With respect and humility.

6. Read Galatians 2:2 in The Message Bible. Name three reasons Paul met with Peter, James, and John privately.
   A. **To share the revelation of the Gospel being preached among the Gentiles.**
   B. **To keep potential ethnic tensions from tainting the Gospel.**
   C. **It was done privately so that if there were any disagreements, it wouldn't become a controversial public issue.**

7. Read Galatians 1:16-17. Do you think Paul was seeking their approval to validate his ministry?
   No.
   Explain:
   He didn't need to because he had the confirmation of his calling from Christ Himself.

8. Read Galatians 1:18, and combining it with Galatians 2:1 how many years had Paul been in the ministry?
   Seventeen years.

9. Read Galatians 2:2. What did Paul say his work and ministry efforts were if the Jerusalem elders disagreed with the Gospel he was preaching?
   That what he had done would have been in vain, for nothing, and a waste.

10. Read Galatians 2:3. Was Titus required to follow the customary Jewish laws and be circumcised?
No. He understood the message of salvation by grace, and he knew that there was nothing he could do to add to what Jesus had accomplished for him.

11. Read Galatians 2:4. How was it known that Titus wasn't circumcised?
There were spies.

12. Read Acts 15:1. What did the legalistic Jews believe the Gentiles must do in order to be saved?
Be circumcised according to the Law of Moses.

13. Read Galatians 2:4. If the deceptive plan of the legalistic Jews of spying on the liberty of Paul and his co-workers had worked, what message would that have sent to the people regarding the Gospel that Paul was preaching?
That it was false.

14. Read Galatians 1:8-9. What is to become of these "false-Christians" who teach that what Jesus did for us in order to be accepted by God was not enough?
_____

15. Read Galatians 2:5. Write out the noted translations regarding Paul's reactions to this covert manipulation.
    A. **Moffat - We refused to yield for a single moment.**
    B. **Living Bible - We didn't listen to them for a single moment.**
    C. **The Message - We didn't give them the time of day.**

16. Read Galatians 2:5 in the Living Bible. Why wouldn't Paul budge, even just a little?
"For we did not want to confuse you into thinking salvation could be earned by the Jewish laws."

17. Read Galatians 2:5 in the Message Bible. What was their reaction to this religious manipulation?
"Don't give it the time of day."

18. Read Hosea 4:6 and Ephesians 4:14. What causes people to be carried away by every wind of doctrine?
Ignorance of God's Word and a lack of knowledge.

19. Read Ephesians 4:11-12. Why were the gifts of the apostles, prophets, evangelists, pastors and teachers given to the church?
    A. **To equip the saints for the work of the ministry.**
    B. **To edify the body of Christ.**

20. Read Ephesians 4:13-15. What is the result of this equipping and edifying?
    - **A. Come to the unity of the faith.**
    - **B. And the knowledge of the Son of God.**
    - **C. Come to be mature, or full-grown.**
    - **D. Measuring up to the stature of Christ.**

21. Read Ephesians 4:14. What is a person considered if he or she is still swayed by the "doctrines of man"?
    A child.

22. Read Ephesians 4:4. What is the result of knowing the truth?
    You will grow up in all things in Him who is the head.

23. Read Galatians 2:6. Was Paul impressed with manly titles or lofty positions?
    No.

24. When dealing with people, what is the most important thing to consider:
    - A. Position and Reputation.
    - **B. Godly Character.**

25. Read Acts 2:11. Does God treat everyone the same?
    Yes.

26. Read Proverbs 16:2 in the Amplified Bible "All the ways of man are pure in his own eyes, but the Lord weighs the spirits (thoughts and intents of the heart.)" What does the Lord weigh?
    The thoughts and intents of the heart.

27. Is it possible to have a good idea, but a wrong motive?
    Yes.

28. Read Acts 15:11. What was the "Gospel for the uncircumcised"?
    By grace through faith, apart form the Law.

29. Read Romans 3:28. What was the "Gospel for the circumcised"?
    By grace through faith, apart form the Law.

30. Read Galatians 2:7-9. As Paul privately and systematically discussed to those of reputation the Gospel he was preaching to the Gentiles (2:2), what did those in the meeting perceive?
    That it was the same Gospel.

31. Read Galatians 2:9. Once Peter, James and John realized Paul and Barnabas were all part of the same team, playing by the same rules, what was their reaction?
    They accepted and encouraged Paul to continue ministering to the Gentiles.

32. Read Ephesians 4:1-6. What are the five ways stated to walk worthy of your calling?
    A. **Be humble.**
    B. **Be gentle.**
    C. **Be patient with one another.**
    D. **Make allowances for each other's faults because of your love.**
    E. **Always keep yourselves united in the Holy Spirit, bind yourselves together in peace.**

33. Read 1 Corinthians 1:10. What did Paul plead with the Corinthians to do?
    A. **That they would all speak the same thing (stop arguing among themselves).**
    B. **That there would be no divisions among them (be in harmony).**
    C. **That they would be perfectly joined together in the same mind (be united in thought).**
    D. **And that they would have the same judgment (be united in purpose).**

34. Read Galatians 2:10. What was Peter's only desire, or request, of Paul?
    To remember the poor.

35. Read James 2:1-4. Should a Christian who claims to have faith in Jesus, shows respect or favor to certain people over others?
    No.

36. Read James 2:8. How is the royal law fulfilled according to this Scripture?
    To love your neighbor as yourself.

37. Read Galatians 2:11-12. Why did Paul confront Peter?
    Because of his actions. He was acting like a hypocrite. Peter was afraid of what some people (the Judaizers) would think of him eating with Gentiles even though God had given him a vision (Acts 11:5-18) and told him that "What God has cleansed you must not call common [or unclean]" (Acts 11:9), concluding that "God had also given the Gentiles the privilege of turning from sin and receiving eternal life" (NLT).

38. Read Galatians 2:7. Why did Paul feel it was necessary to confront him?
    Because God had entrusted them both with the Gospel of grace.

39. Read Galatians 2:4. What was Peter experiencing with the Gentiles before the "religious" Judaizers came to town?
    His Christian liberty.

40. Read Galatians 2:12. What compelled Peter to hypocrisy?
    The fear of man.

41. Read Galatians 2:13. What was the consequence of Peter's hypocrisy?
    The other Jewish Christians followed Peter's hypocrisy, and even Barnabas was influenced to join them.

42. Read Galatians 2:13. Why did Paul make it a point to mention that even Barnabas got carried away with their hypocrisy?
Because Barnabas had spent much time with Paul and heard him minister the truth. Even though he knew what was right, he was influenced to follow Peter's hypocrisy.

43. If you sway from the truth even a little, what effect can it have on those around you?
It will send the wrong message regarding the truth of the Gospel.

44. Read Galatians 2:5. What was Paul's response to the pressure of man-pleasing Judaizers?
Do not listen to them, do not yield to them, not even for an hour.

45. Read Galatians 2:14. What was Paul's concern, regarding their hypocrisy, which was revealed by their actions?
    A. He was mad, because he wasn't invited.
    B. The motive behind their actions wasn't right.
    C. He and Barnabas already had dinner plans.

46. Read Galatians 1:8-9. What is Paul's stand regarding presenting the "true Gospel"?
If any other gospel is preached, let that person be accursed.

47. Read Titus 1:10-11. What were the Judaizers' motive behind their idle talk, deception and distorted teachings?
Dishonest gain, that is, they only wanted money.

48. Read Titus 1:16. What happens when a person talks the talk but doesn't walk the walk?
They are disqualified, being unfit for doing the good works God wanted them to do. They will turn people away from receiving the Gospel.

49. Complete the cliché. "**PRACTICE** what you preach."

50. Read Philippians 3:4-5. Was Paul a real Jew?
Yes.

51. Read Galatians 2:16. What must every individual do in order to be justified before God?
Believe in and trust Jesus Christ as the one and only Lord and Savior.

52. Read Romans 3:20. Can anyone be made right by doing what the Law demands?
No.

53. Read Romans 8:23-28. How are we made right with God?
By His grace through faith. Not by the Law or by trying to be good.

54. Read Galatians 2:16. If you are "declared righteous" by the faith of Jesus Christ, how do you make yourself a transgressor or Law breaker?
By trying to keep the Law.

55. Read Romans 8:3. Can we ever keep the Law to be righteous?
No. Jesus died for the broken Law that we could not keep. "The law of Moses could not save us, because of our sinful nature. But God put into effect a different plan to save us. He sent his own son in a human body like ours, except that ours are sinful. God destroyed sin's control over us by giving His son as a sacrifice for our sins" (Romans 8:3, NLT).

56. Read James 2:10-11. Is the law a complete system that must be kept and obeyed in its entirety?
Yes, but we cannot keep it, we fail every time.

57. Read Galatians 2:17-18. Does Christ promote sin by releasing us from the bondage that a legalistic system held us in?
No. Of course not! He whom the Son sets free is free indeed (John 8:36)!

58. Read 2 Corinthians 3:5. Is your sufficiency from YOURSELF or **GOD**?

59. Read 2 Corinthians 3:6. What has a believer been qualified for and made a minister of?
The New Covenant.

60. Read 2 Corinthians 3:6. What does the "letter," or Law, do?
It kills.

61. Read 2 Corinthians 3:6. What does the Spirit give?
Life.

62. Read Hebrews 8:7. Was the first covenant faultless?
No. If it had been, then there would be no need for a second covenant to replace it.

63. Read Hebrew 8:8-12. Was the Old Covenant of the Law meant to survive?
No. God Himself found fault with it and wanted to relpace it. So, it was replaced.

64. Read Galatians 2:19. According to this verse what happened to us through the Law?
We died to the Law by being crucified with Christ.

65. Read Romans 7:4. If you were crucified with Christ, can the Law any longer have power over you?
66. **No. It was through the Law that I was released from the Law. I am now united to Christ being raised from the dead with Him.**

67. Read Galatians 2:20. What does this verse say has happened to you through Christ?
It says that I was crucified with Him.

68. Read Galatians 2:20. The crucifixion and resurrection of Jesus brings us new life. According to this verse, who lives in us, and how are we able to now live this life?
When we believe, Jesus Christ lives in us. We can live this way, in our earthly bodies, by trusting in the Son of God.

69. Read Galatians 2:20 in The Message Bible. What four things happen when you are crucified with Christ?
    A. Ego is no longer central.
    B. It is no longer important to appear righteous.
    C. No longer seek man's approval or acceptance.
    D. I'm no longer driven to impress God.

70. Read Galatians 2:21. What happens when a person treats God's gift of grace as something of minor importance, setting it aside and invalidating it?
    It frustrates and nullifies the grace of God.

71. Read Galatians 3:21. Can the Law make us right with God?
    No. Only the sacrifice that Jesus made can make us right with God.

72. Read Romans 5:17. When we receive God's abundant grace and the gift of righteousness we will:
    A. Declare that Christ did not die in vain.
    B. Reign in life by Jesus Christ.
    C. Have a living and vital relationship with God.
    D. All of the above

73. Read 1 Corinthians 1:18. What is the message of the cross to those who are perishing?
    It is foolishness.

74. What is the message of the cross to those who are being saved?
    It is the power of God.

Galatians 3:1-29
Discipleship Commentary

....

Galatians 3:1

O foolish Galatians, who hath bewitched you, that ye should not obey the truth, before whose eyes Jesus Christ hath been evidently set forth, crucified among you? (KJV)

Oh, foolish Galatians! What magician has hypnotized you and cast an evil spell upon you? For you used to see meaning of Jesus Christ's death as clearly as though I had waved a placard before you with a picture on it of Christ dying on the cross. (LB)

You foolish Galatians! Who has bewitched you – you who saw Jesus Christ publicly pictured as crucified? (Beck)

Are you people in Galatia mad? Has someone put a spell on you, in spite of the plain explanation you have had of the crucifixion of Jesus Christ? (TJB)

You crazy Galatians! Did someone put a hex on you? Have you taken leave of your senses? Something crazy has happened, for it's obvious that you no longer have the crucified Jesus in clear focus in your lives. His sacrifice on the Cross was certainly set before you clearly enough. (TM)

(Gal. 3:1) Paul begins this chapter with the statement, "O foolish Galatians!" "Foolish" carries the idea of someone who is seeing things from a distorted viewpoint and has lost the divine perspective.

The reason that the Galatians had lost the divine viewpoint is because of spiritual bewitchment. Can a born-again, Spirit-filled Christian be bewitched? The Galatians were, like victims of an evil spell. What happened? Their spiritual eyes were re-directed away from grace and unto Law, so that in a real sense, they had fallen from grace (Gal. 5:4).

The phrase "before whose eyes Jesus Christ hath been evidently set forth crucified among you" was a term in Paul's day that had to do with the writing or posting of a public announcement on something similar to a billboard. Paul is saying that you came to saving faith in Christ on the basis of Christ and Him crucified; it was so clear to you. Now why have you embraced a different message?

Galatians 3:2

This only would I learn of you, Received ye the Spirit by the works of the law, or by the hearing of faith? (KJV)

I want to ask you only this one thing: Did you receive the Spirit by doing what the law commands, or by believing the message you heard? (Wms)

I want to know only one thing. How were you given God's Spirit? Was it by obeying the Law of Moses or by hearing about Christ and having faith in Him? (CEV)

Let me put this question to you: How did your new life begin? Was it by working your heads off to please God? Or was it by responding to God's Message to you? (TM)

(Gal. 3:2) Paul is saying, "Oh, Galatians, even though I instructed you in the way of the Gospel and was your teacher, this is what I want to learn from you: Did you receive the Holy Spirit because I instructed you to observe the Law of Moses? Or did I instruct you in the Gospel of Christ and you believed it? Obviously you received the gift of the Holy Spirit by faith!"

Galatians 3:3

Are you so foolish? Having begun in the Spirit, are ye now made perfect by the flesh? (KJV)

Are you so foolish? After beginning with the Spirit, are you now trying to attain your goal by human effort? (NIV)

You began with the Spirit. Are you trying to continue it by your own power? (SE)

Are you foolish enough to end in outward observances what you began in the Spirit? (TJB)

Are you going to continue this craziness? For only crazy people would think they could complete by their own efforts what was begun by God. If you weren't smart enough or strong enough to begin it, how do you suppose you could perfect it? (TM)

(Gal. 3:3) Paul goes on to say, "You began this race with the Spirit's power; you're now trying to end it with human effort, i.e., self-effort. You began with dependence upon God's Spirit, i.e., faith; you have now turned to the works of the Law for justification and Christian living (Rom. 7). How could you be so foolish?"

The New International Version translates "made perfect by the flesh" by the phrase "to attain your goal by human effort."

Galatians 3:4

Have ye suffered so many things in vain? If it be yet in vain. (KJV)

You have suffered so much for the Gospel. Now are you going to just throw it all overboard? I can hardly believe it. (LB)

Did you go through this whole painful learning process for nothing? It is not yet a total loss, but it certainly will be if you keep this up! (TM)

(Gal. 3:4) The Galatians had suffered many things for the sake of the Gospel (Acts 13:45, 50, 14:2, 5, 19, and 22). Now they are ready to throw it all overboard by accepting a different gospel, a different message. It would be like a politician taking a stand against abortion and suffering much because of it. But now he has turned pro-abortion. He's suffered so much in vain. Paul says of the Galatians, "I can hardly believe what you've done" (LB)!

Galatians 3:5

He therefore that ministereth to you the Spirit, and worketh miracles among you, doeth he it by the works of the law, or by the hearing of faith? (KJV)

Does God give you the Spirit because you follow law? Does God work miracles among you because you follow the law? It is because you heard and believed. (SE)

Answer this question: Does the God who lavishly provides you with His own presence, His Holy Spirit, working things in your lives you could never do for yourselves, does he do these things because of your strenuous moral striving or because you trust him to do them in you? (TM)

(Gal. 3:5) The "He" in this verse may be the Apostle Paul, but more correctly, it is God Himself who supplies the Spirit and works miracles among the Galatians. God does so on the basis of faith, not by the works of the Law or human effort. "Peter...answered unto the people, ye men of Israel, why marvel ye at this? Or why look ye so earnestly on us, as though by our own power or holiness we made this man to walk?...His name (Jesus Christ), through faith in His name, hath made this man strong, whom ye see and know: yea, the faith which is by Him hath given him this perfect soundness in the presence of you all" (Acts 3:12, 16).

Galatians 3:6
Even as Abraham believed God, and it was accounted to him for righteousness. (KJV)

The Scriptures say the same thing about Abraham: "Abraham believed God, and so God declared him a righteous man. – Gen 15:6 (SE)

Don't these things happen among you just as they happened with Abraham? He believed God, and that act of belief was turned into a life that was right with God. (TM)

(Gal. 3:6) In verses 1-5 of this chapter, Paul has been appealing to the previous experience of the Galatians. It was through faith that God supplied them the Spirit, worked miracles among them, etc.

Paul is now introducing the Old Testament example of Abraham being put right with God through faith. He will continue this reasoning until the end of chapter 4. His main point will emphasize that we also are made right with God through faith in Jesus Christ.

The Judaizers had claimed the Old Testament scriptures to be on their side against Paul's message of Grace. Paul is now going back some 430 years further than Moses to consider Abraham. Abraham was considered the father of the Jewish nation, not Moses. Paul's point is that Abraham was justified by faith not law, so also will his descendants be saved in the same manner. Paul is quoting Genesis 15:6 in the Old Testament to prove that Abraham was justified through faith in the promises of God (Genesis 15:1-5). The promise that Abraham was given was concerning a son (a seed). This was the content of his faith. The moment Abraham believed, God put to his account something that he did not have before, i.e., righteousness.

This scripture is quoted again in Romans 4:3 as an example of justification by faith (Rom. 4:1-11, 18-25).

Galatians 3:7
Know ye therefore that they which are of faith;, the same are the children of Abraham. (KJV)

So you see, it is the men of faith who are the real descendants of Abraham. (Wms)

Is it not obvious to you that persons who put their trust in Christ (not persons who put their trust in the law!) are like Abraham: children of faith? (TM)

(Gal. 3:7) Paul is stating, "Don't you Galatians realize that the real children of Abraham are those who have the same characteristics that Abraham had, i.e., faith and reliance upon God" (Rom 2:28-29)?

Galatians 3:8
And the scripture, foreseeing that God would justify the heathen through faith, preached before the gospel unto Abraham, saying, In thee shall all nations be blessed. (KJV)

What's more, the Scriptures looked forward to this time when God would save the Gentiles also, through their faith. God told Abraham about this long ago when he said, "I will bless those in every nation who trust Me as you do." And so it is: all who trust in Christ share the same blessing Abraham received. (LB)

The Scripture foresaw that God would justify the Gentiles by faith, and announced the gospel in advance to Abraham: "All nations will be blessed through you." (NIV)

It was all laid out beforehand in Scripture that God would set things right with non-Jews by faith. Scripture anticipated this in the promise to Abraham: "All nations will be blessed in you." (TM)

(Gal.3:8) The Scriptures "foresaw" that God would justify the Gentiles through faith. The word "foreseeing" carries the ideas of "predicting or declaring ahead of time" this good news of the Gospel. The scripture that is cited is Genesis 12:3, in which God said that Abraham would be used in bringing blessing to all people on the earth. This blessing would ultimately come through Abraham's seed, Jesus Christ.

Galatians 3:9
So then they which be of faith are blessed with faithful Abraham. (KJV)

So then those who are of faith are blessed with believing Abraham. (NKJV)

All people who believe are blessed in the same way that Abraham was blessed for his faith. (SE)

> **So those now who live by faith are blessed along with Abraham, who lived by faith – this is no new doctrine! (TM)**

(Gal. 3:9) Abraham believed and was blessed. So, also, those who believe are blessed as Abraham was. Part of the blessing of our spiritual inheritance is described in Romans 4:6-11. We are blessed with the same things that Abraham was blessed with—justification through faith and the promise of the Holy Spirit (Gal. 3:14).

Galatians 3:10

> **For as many as are of the works of the law are under the curse: for it is written, Cursed is every one that continueth not in all things which are written in the book of the law and do them. (KJV)**

> **Yes, and those who depend on the Jewish laws to save them are under God's curse, for the Scriptures point out very clearly, "Cursed is everyone who at any time breaks a single one of these laws that are written in God's Book of the Law." (LB)**

> **But people who depend on following the law to make them right are under condemnation, because it is written, " A person must do everything which is written in the book of the law. If he does not always obey those things, then that person is under condemnation!" (Deut. 27:26) (SE)**

> **And that means that anyone who tries to live by his own effort, independent of God, is doomed to failure. Scripture backs this up: "Utterly cursed is every person who fails to carry out every detail written in the Book of the Law." (TM)**

(Gal. 3:10) The two key words in this passage are "continueth" and "all," from the statement, "Cursed is every one that *[continueth]* not in *[all]* things which are written in the book of the law to do them." The Judaizers claimed justification and blessing on anyone who obeyed the Law. But in reality, the Law brought a curse and God's wrath (Rom. 4:15). The curse lay dormant as long as the Law was obeyed perfectly, but as soon as it was violated its curse came into effect (Deut. 27:26, 28:15-68). A curse is that which invokes calamity or evil. It's the opposite of "blessing." "Blessings" are a gift of divine favor. Justification by Law, either wholly or in part, is that which brings on divine disapproval, wrath, and ultimate alienation from God. "Ye are severed from Christ ye (that) would be justified by the law" (Gal 5:4, ASV).

Galatians 3:11

But that no man is justified by the law in the sight of God, it is evident: for, The just shall live by faith. (KJV)

Now it is evident that no man is justified before God by the law; for "He who through faith is righteous shall live" (RSV)

Now it is evident that through the law no man is brought into right standing with God, for "The man in right standing with God, will live by faith." (Wms)

The obvious impossibility of carrying out such a moral program should make it plain that no one can sustain a relationship with God that way. The person who lives in right relationship with God does it by embracing what God arranges for him. Doing things for God is the opposite of entering into what God does for you. Habakkuk had it right: "The person who believes God, is set right by God – and that's the real life." (TM)

(Gal. 3:11) If the Law brought a curse (v. 10), then it is evident that it cannot bring justification. That no man was ever justified by the Law is made plain by the scripture itself in Habakkuk 2:4. "There are two ways of rendering the quotation: either 'the just shall live by faith' (NAB, J.B. Phil), or 'the just through faith shall live' (TEV, NEB, RSV)" (*USB Handbook*, p. 64). Faith is what imparted spiritual life, not works of the Law.

Galatians 3:12

And the law is not of faith: but, The man that doeth them shall live in them. (KJV)

The law is not based on faith. Instead, "A person who wants to find life by following these things must do the things the law says." Lev. 18:5 (SE)

How different from this way of faith is the way of law which says that a man is saved by obeying every law of God, without one slip. (LB)

Rule keeping does not naturally evolve into living by faith, but only perpetuates itself in more and more rule keeping, a fact observed in Scripture: "The one who does these things [rule keeping] continues to live by them." (TM)

(Gal.3:12) When Paul is speaking about faith, he is also implying grace. He now states that "the law is not of faith" or grace. Romans 4:4 states, "Now to him that worketh [the principle of law] is the reward [or wages] not reckoned of grace [favor], but of debt [an obligation]." In other words, under Law, you get what you deserve, under grace, you receive God's favor. Romans 11:6 also states, "And if by grace, then it is no more of works: otherwise grace is no more grace." Faith receives what grace has provided. The Law is not of faith and gives you what is due (a curse and spiritual death).

Paul is now quoting Leviticus 18:5, which he also quotes in Romans 10:5 (Rom. 10:3-10). In Romans 10, Paul makes the contrast of the Law saying, "DO and you shall live," with faith saying, "DONE," and receiving what grace has provided (salvation for all mankind).

Galatians 3:13

Christ hath redeemed us from the curse of the law, being made a curse for us: for it is written, Cursed is every one that hangeth on a tree: (KJV)

Christ ransomed us from the curse pronounced in the Law, by taking the curse on himself for us, for Scripture says – 'Cursed is any one who is hanged on a tree.' (TCNT)

But Christ has bought us out from under the doom of that impossible system by taking the curse for our wrongdoing upon Himself. For it is written in the Scripture, "Anyone who is hanged on a tree is cursed: [as Jesus was hung upon a wooden cross]." (LB)

Christ redeemed us from that self-defeating, cursed life by absorbing it completely into Himself. Do you remember the Scripture that says, "Cursed is everyone who hangs on a tree"? That is what happened when Jesus was nailed to the Cross: He became a curse, and at the same time dissolved the curse. (TM)

(Gal. 3:13) Any failure to obey the Law brought on the Law's curse (Deut. 28:15-68). Christ has redeemed us from the curse of disobedience to the Law. The Law could bring "blessing" if obeyed or "cursing" if disobeyed.

Paul cites Deuteronomy 21:23 to show that justice was satisfied when Jesus died for the Law we broke, thus paying its penalty and bearing its curse. There is no condemnation awaiting us from the Law, for we died in Him.

There are three basic Greek words for REDEEMED.
1. AGORAZO, which means, "to buy in the slave market" (we were slaves to the law).
2. EX-AGORAZO, which means, "to buy OUT OF the slave market" (it would remove us out from under the principle of the law).
3. LUTROO means, "to SET FREE or RELEASE by a payment" (Christ's death paid in full the justice the law demanded).

We are now free from the Law to be in union with another—Jesus Christ (Rom. 7:4). What the Law was to the Jew (they thought it was eternal life), Jesus is to the believer. Jesus said, "Search the scriptures (Old Testament law and prophets); for in them ye [THINK YE HAVE ETERNAL LIFE:] and they are they which testify of me" (John. 5:39). Jesus Christ has replaced the Law by Himself becoming the full manifestation of the will of God (Heb. 1:1-2).

Galatians 3:14
That the blessing of Abraham might come on the Gentiles through Jesus Christ; that we might receive the promise of the Spirit through faith. (KJV)

God's purpose is therefore plain: that the blessing promised to Abraham might reach the Gentiles through Jesus Christ, and the promise of the Spirit might become ours by faith. (J.B. Phil)

And now, because of that, the air is cleared and we can see that Abraham's blessing is present and available for non-Jews, too. We are all able to receive God's life, His Spirit, in and with us by believing – just the way Abraham received it. (TM)

(Gal. 3:14) You can't be cursed and blessed at the same time. A curse is the opposite of a blessing. Christ first removed the curse of a broken Law by bearing its penalty so that by receiving the Law's curse and punishment as our substitute, the blessings of grace and faith that Abraham received can be ours. The blessing (divine favor) of Abraham is manifest to us in at least two ways:

1. By our faith in Christ accounted to us for righteousness (Rom. 4:5-9).
2. We have the indwelling, abiding presence of the Holy Spirit in our hearts by faith (Gal. 3:14).

Galatians 3:15
Brethren, I speak after the manner of men; Though it be but a man's covenant, yet if it be confirmed, no man disannulleth, or addeth thereto. (KJV)

Brethren, I speak after the manner of men: Though it be but a man's covenant, yet when it hath been confirmed, no one maketh it void, or addeth thereto. (ASV)

To give a human example, brethren: No one annuls even a man's will, or adds to it, once it has been ratified. (RSV)

Brothers, let me give you an example: A man writes a will. After the will is made legal, no one else may change that will or add to it, and no one can ignore it. (SE)

Dear brothers, even in everyday life a promise made by one man to another, if it is written down and signed, cannot be changed. He cannot decide afterward to do something else instead. (LB)

Friends, let me give you an example from everyday affairs of the free life I am talking about. Once a person's will has been ratified, no one else can annul it or add to it. (TM)

(Gal. 3:15) Paul is saying, "I'm going to use a human illustration. If a man's covenant, contract, or agreement was drawn up and ratified, i.e., you have done whatever is necessary to give it legal force, then no man can break the agreement or add conditions to it."

If it was a contract to build a house for $75,000, the contractor can't come in and say, "I'm not making enough money on this," and write in $100,000.00 on the contract. Nor can the buyer add in an extra room at the same price.

Galatians 3:16

Now to Abraham and his seed were the promises made. He saith not, And to seeds, as of many; but as of one, And to thy seed, which is Christ. (KJV)

The promises were spoken to Abraham and to his seed. The Scripture does not say "and to seeds," meaning many people, but "and to your seed," meaning one person, who is Christ. (NIV)

Now, God gave some promises to Abraham and his Child. And notice that it doesn't say the promises were to his children, as it would if all his sons – all the Jews – were being spoken of, but to his Child – and that, of course, means Christ. (LB)

Now, the promises were made to Abraham and to his descendant. You will observe that Scripture, in the careful language of a legal document, does not say "to descendants," referring to everybody in general, but "to your descendant" (the noun, note, is singular), referring to Christ. (TM)

(Gal. 3:16) Paul has been arguing since verse 15 that the promise, or covenant, given to Abraham is still in force (because no man can add to or take away from a legal covenant).

The promise, or covenant, was made with Abraham and his "seed" (singular) (Gen. 12:2-3, 13:14-15, 15:1,5-6, 18, 17:2-7; Rom. 4:6-9, 13-14, 22-25; and Gal. 3:14, 22, 29). The promises were not given to Abraham and his "seeds" (referring to the Jewish people, his descendants), but to his "seed," his ONE descendant, which is Christ. "The promises...spoken to Abraham and to his seed...found fulfillment in Christ and are in effect forever" (BKC, p. 598).

The Greek word "seed" is "SPERMA," which means, "the seed, i.e. the grain or kernel which contains within itself the germ of the future plants" (Thayer's Greek Lexicon). Paul is going to later argue that believers were the future plants, so to speak, which were in the one seed, Christ. "Thus to Abraham personally and to all those who by faith in Christ are brought into salvation, were the promises made" (*Wuest Word Studies Volume 1*, p. 101, Gal. 3:29). God's promise of justification through faith was given long before the introduction of the law.

Since the promise was made to his seed, Christ, the only way to participate in the promise is through Christ. This is why the promise is of no effect through the Law, because the Law bypasses Christ. If you bypass Christ, you forego the promise.

Galatians 3:17-18

And this I say, that the covenant, that was confirmed before of God in Christ, the law, which was four hundred and thirty years after, cannot disannul, that it should make the promise of none effect. For if the inheritance be of the law, it is no more of promise: but God gave it to Abraham by promise. (KJV)

What I mean is this: The law, introduced 430 years later, does not set aside the covenant previously established by God and thus do away with the promise. For if inheritance depends on the law, then it no longer depends on a promise; but God in his grace gave it to Abraham through a promise. (NIV)

Here's what I am trying to say: God's promise to save through faith—and God wrote this promise down and signed it—could not be canceled or changed four hundred and thirty years later when God gave the Ten Commandments. If obeying those laws could save us, then it is obvious that this would be a different way of gaining God's favor than Abraham's way, for he simply accepted God's promise. (LB)

That is what I mean God made out a will to Abraham, promising to do the things he told Abraham. Law came 430 years after the will was made, but it did not change God's promise to Abraham. Can following law give us the things, which God promised? If we could receive those things by following law, then it is not God's promise, which brings those things. But God freely gave to Abraham through the promise made. (SE)

This is the way I interpret this: a will, earlier ratified by God, is not annulled by an addendum attached 430 years later, thereby negating the promise of the will. No, this addendum, with its instructions and regulations, has nothing to do with the promised inheritance in the will. (TM)

(Gal. 3:18) Paul is now stating what his words really mean as he began his argument in verse 15. If a man's covenant cannot be added to or taken away from, then God's covenant of promise to save men through faith in Christ cannot be affected through the introduction of the Law some 430 years after God's promise.

In verse 18, Paul says that if God's blessings (inheritance) depend on keeping the Law, then they can't be given by a promise. But God blessed Abraham simply because He promised to do so.

The Living Bible paraphrases verse 17-18 in the following way: "Here's what I am trying to say: God's promise to save through faith – and God wrote this promise down and signed it – could not be canceled or changed four hundred and thirty years later when God gave the Ten Commandments. If obeying those laws could save us, then it is obvious that this would be a different way of gaining God's favor than Abraham's way, for he *simply accepted God's promise.*"

Galatians 3:19

Wherefore then serveth the law? It was added because of transgressions, till the seed should come to whom the promise was made; and it was ordained by angels in the hand of a mediator. (KJV)

What, then, was the purpose of the law? It was added because of transgressions until the Seed to whom the promise referred had come. The law was put into effect through angels by a mediator. (NIV)

Therefore, what was the purpose of the law? The Law was given to show people the difference between right and wrong. It continued until the special descendant of Abraham came. The law was given through angels. The angels used Moses as a go-between to give the law to men. (SE)

Well then, why were the laws given? They were added after the promise was given, to show men how guilty they are of breaking God's laws. But this system of law was to last only until the coming of Christ, the Child to whom God's promise was made. (And there is further difference. God gave his laws to angels to give to Moses, who then gave them to the people; (LB)

What is the point, then, of the law, the attached addendum? It was a thoughtful addition to the original covenant promises made to Abraham. The purpose of the law was to keep a sinful people in the way of salvation until Christ (the descendant) came, inheriting the promises and distributing them to us. Obviously this law was not a firsthand encounter with God. It was arranged by angelic messengers through a middleman, Moses. (TM)

(Gal. 3:19) If the Law was not given to save us either partly or wholly, then why was it given? It was added to the covenant of grace to define transgression, to show the real nature of sin and wrongdoing so that we would be ready to hear about the covenant of grace (Gal. 3:24). It was to remain valid and in force until the coming of the one true descendant of Abraham, i.e., Christ. The Law was from God and given to angels (Heb. 2:2, Acts 7:38) to give to Moses who gave it to the people.

So we can say the Law was only a temporary measure. How temporary? "Till" Christ should come. God was twice removed from its recipients (God-angels-Moses-the people). Whereas in the covenant of faith, God alone walked between the pieces of cut animal (Gen. 15) to establish a direct covenant with Abraham's seed, Jesus Christ (while Abraham slept). This establishes the fact that this covenant is unconditional and eternal, because the two parties involved are God the Father and Abraham's seed, Jesus Christ. Man can't mess this one up; it's of promise, whereas the covenant of Law is conditional based upon men's ability to obey.

Galatians 3:20
Now a mediator is not a mediator of one, but God is one (KJV)

A go-between is not needed when there is only one side; God is only one side. (SE)

But when God gave his promise to Abraham, he did it by Himself alone, without angels or Moses as go-betweens. (LB)

But if there is a middleman as there was at Sinai, then the people are not dealing directly with God, are they? But the original promise is the *direct* blessing of God, received by faith. (TM)

(Gal. 3:20) "Now a mediator is not a mediator of one." The word "mediator" literally means, "to be in the middle of midst." It carries the idea of one who intervenes between two or more and acts as a go-between (*Wuest Word Studies, Volume 1*, p. 106). Paul's main point here is that the covenant of promise is superior to the Law, because under the Law, go-betweens were used in dealing with the people, whereas under grace, God dealt directly with Abraham.

The thought about "God is one" apparently means God acted alone, directly with Abraham.

Galatians 3:21-22

Is the law then against the promises of God? God forbid: for if there had been a law given which could have given life, verily righteousness should have been by the law. But the Scripture hath concluded all under sin, that the promise by faith of Jesus Christ might be given to them that believe (KJV)

Therefore, does this mean that the law is against God's promises" If there were a law which could give men life, then we could truly be made right by following law. However this cannot be true, because the scriptures showed that all people are bound by sin, so that the promise would be given to people through faith – to those who believe in Jesus Christ (SE)

Is the law, therefore, opposed to the promises of God? Absolutely not! For if a law had been given that could impart life, then righteousness would certainly have come by the law. But the Scripture declares that the whole world is a prisoner of sin, so that what was promised, being given through faith in Jesus Christ, might be given to those who believe. (NIV)

If such is the case, is the law, then, an anti-promise, a negation of God's will for us? Not at all. Its purpose was to make obvious to everyone that we are, in ourselves, out of right relationship with God, and therefore to show us the futility of devising some religious system for getting by on our own efforts what we can only get by waiting in faith for God to complete His promise. For if any kind of rule keeping had power to create life in us, we would certainly have gotten it by this time. (TM)

(Gal.3:21-22) Because of all that has been said in the negative concerning the law, if I were asked the question, "is the law against the promises of God" I would probably reply, "Yes!" But notice Paul's reply was, "NO! God forbid, may it never be true."

You see, "Paul is able to give a negative answer to this question because he not only allows that the law has a function, but that function is even related to the fulfillment of God's promise. Already he has said that the law functions as showing what wrongdoing is (v.19), and later he takes up other functions of the law: as teacher (vv. 23-25) and as guardian (4:1). But the function of the law is not the same as the function of the promise. The function of the promise is to bring LIFE. If the law could do that, then it would be competing with the promise. But the law cannot bring life, because it was not given for such a purpose" (*USB Handbook*, p. 77)

In the Greek, there is no definite article before "Law," which indicates that Paul is speaking about religious Law in general. No religious law has the power to bring forth life and produce the right-standing that God requires for salvation. Justification does not, and cannot, come by Law.

The Old Testament scripture had "concluded all under sin" (Rom. 3:9-20). This phrase "concluded all under sin" is a technical term used for prisoners being confined or imprisoned. Paul is speaking of all mankind being imprisoned and subject to sin and its bondage. This could be translated "everybody in the world is controlled by his strong desire to sin" (*USB Handbook*, p. 79). Promised righteousness and deliverance from sin come not by observance of the Law but through faith in Jesus Christ (Rom. 7:24-25, 11:32).

Galatians 3:23

But before faith came, we were kept under the law, shut up unto the faith which should afterwards be revealed. (KJV)

Before this faith came, we were held prisoners by the law, locked up until faith should be revealed. (NIV)

Before this faith came, we were held in check by law. We had no freedom until God revealed to us the way of faith which was coming. (SE)

Until the time when we were mature enough to respond freely in faith to the living God, we were carefully surrounded and protected by the Mosaic Law. (TM)

(Gal. 3:23) "But before faith came" is not speaking of faith in general, such as the faith Abraham exercised 430 years before the Law. This is faith described in verse 22 as "faith in Jesus Christ." Men have always been saved by faith, but the content of their faith has been somewhat varied. Verse 25 reveals that "faith has come," i.e., the understanding of faith in the Lord Jesus Christ for salvation has come.

"We were kept under the law, shut up" waiting for saving faith in Christ to be revealed. The word "kept" in the Greek carries the idea of a jailer who has imprisoned us under guilt and condemnation. The consciousness of sin is always present, and we are always looking inwardly at ourselves. It is only faith in Jesus Christ that has the key to unlock the door to the Law's harsh imprisonment of guilt and condemnation (1 Cor. 15:56-57).

Galatians 3:24

Wherefore the law was our schoolmaster to bring us unto Christ, that we might be justified by faith. (KJV)

Thus, even as the slave who leads a child to the house of the schoolmaster, so the Law has led us to [our teacher] Christ, that by Faith we might be justified. (Con)

So that the Law has proved a tutor to discipline us for Christ, that through faith we may be justified. (Wey)

Or, to change the metaphor, the Law was like a strict governess in charge of us until we went to the school of Christ and learned to be justified by faith in Him. (J.B. Phil)

The law was like those Greek tutors, with which you are familiar, who escort children to school and protect them from danger or distraction, making sure the children will really get to the place they set out for. (TM)

(Gal. 3:24) The Law is now stated to be our "schoolmaster," "PAIDAGOGOS" in the Greek, and described a slave in either Greek or Roman households whose job it was to conduct a young child to and from school (to the real teacher), as well as to supervise the life and morals of the child until he or she reached maturity. Although the schoolmaster may instruct, their real job was to supervise by strict enforcement of rules and regulation. So until Christ came, the Law was like someone trying to make us behave.

Galatians 3:25
But after that faith is come, we are no longer under a schoolmaster. (KJV)

Now that faith has come, we are no longer under the supervision of the law. (NIV)

The way of faith has come. Therefore, we do not live under law anymore. (SE)

But now you have arrived at your destination: By faith in Christ you are in direct relationship with God. (TM)

(Gal. 3:25) Paul is now stating that the Law has served its function. We are no longer under the Law that would bring guilt and condemnation. We are now under the Savior, Christ Himself.

Galatians 3:26
For ye are all the children of God by faith in Christ Jesus. (KJV)

(Gal. 3:26) We are no longer young children supervised by the "PAIDAGOGOS" (schoolmaster). WE now have liberty, privilege, and rights as full-grown children. The Law said in a figurative manner: "Go to bed at 8:00 pm, look both ways before crossing the street, eat your vegetables, brush your teeth," etc. As full-grown sons and daughters, we have much more freedom—not the freedom to indulge in the lusts of the flesh, but to walk in love before God and man. Our responsibility is directly related to the relationship we have to the One God, who loves us, and to the ones we love.

Galatians 3:27

For as many of you as have been baptized into Christ have put on Christ. (KJV)

Your baptism in Christ was not just washing you up for a fresh start. It also involved dressing you in an adult faith wardrobe—Christ's life, the fulfillment of God's original promise. (TM)

(Gal.32:27) "The word BAPTIZO primarily has to do with identification. It was a term that was used in the first century for dipping a light colored garment into dye that was, let's say, scarlet. Once the fabric was dipped into the scarlet dye, it would be changed in its identity from its original color to scarlet. The act of dipping it, resulting in changing its identity, was called BAPTIZO. It was the Greek term from which we get our English word BAPTISM" (*The Grace Awakening*, by Charles Swindoll, p. 177).

I was once "in Adam," I am now "in Christ." My identity changed through faith in Him, when I was baptized into Christ by the power of the Holy Spirit.

Galatians 3:28

There is neither Jew nor Greek, there is neither bond nor free, there is neither male nor female: for ye are all one in Christ Jesus. (KJV)

There can be neither Jew nor Greek, there can be neither bond nor free, there can be no male and female; for ye are all one man in Christ Jesus. (ASV)

In Christ's family there can be no division into Jew and non-Jew, slave and free, male and female. Among us you are all equal. That is, we are all in a common relationship with Jesus Christ. (TM)

(Gal. 3:28) Distinctions created by religious Law that separated Jew and Gentile, male and female, etc., no longer exist in Christ Jesus (Eph. 2:13-16). Through union with Christ Jesus, we have all been made one. The "one new man," the body of Christ, is joined together by faith in Christ Jesus (Eph. 1:22-23).

Galatians 3:29

And if ye be Christ's, then are ye Abraham's seed, and heirs according to the promise. (KJV)

And now that we are Christ's we are the true descendants of Abraham, and all of God's promises to him belong to us. (LB)

(Gal. 3:29) Going back to verse 16, we discover that promises were made to Abraham and his seed, Christ. Christ was participating in the covenant actually as our representative. The promises were made to Abraham and Christ, but Christ had no need of being justified through faith. Therefore, as our representative, the promise was made to Him for us who are "in Him." We are also guaranteed the success of the covenant (we can't mess it up), because the promise was made to Christ (we receive the benefits of being "in Him").

Galatians 3:1-29
Discipleship Questions

1. Read Galatians 3:1. Was the meaning of Christ's crucifixion and death presented clearly to the Galatians? _____

2. In Galatians 3:1, why was Paul thinking the Galatians had been bewitched? _____

3. Read Ephesians 2:8-9. What was the Gospel they first believed? _____

4. Read John 8:31-32. What did Jesus say knowing the truth does for a person who abides in His Word? _____

5. In Galatians 3:1 why was Paul baffled over what the Galatians had chosen to believe? Read Romans 8:2. _____

6. Read Galatians 3:2. How did the Galatians receive the Spirit?
   A. By keeping the Law.
   B. By faith in Christ.

7. According to Romans 10:17 how does faith come? _____

8. Referring to the other translations and paraphrases noted in the commentary, what are other ways to say, "made perfect by the flesh"?

   NIV - _____

   SE - _____

   TJB - _____

9. Read Ephesians 2:8-9. How is a person saved? _____

10. According to Ephesians 2:8-9 is salvation a gift or do we have to earn it by our works?

11. Read Romans 4:4-5. When a person is employed their wages are not a gift but earned. Can we earn righteousness by the good works that we do? _____

12. What does this truth about God justifying the ungodly reveal about the "getting what you deserve" theory. _____

13. Read Galatians 2:21 and Galatians 3:4. What is the common denominator that causes what Christ did and the things the Galatians suffered when they first believed to be in vain? _____

14. Read Galatians 3:4. Why is it true that the suffering the Galatians endured for standing up for the true Gospel would be in vain? _____

15. Read Galatians 3:4. If you have endured persecution for the sake of the gospel and then compromised the Word of God, what becomes of the good that was done prior? _____

16. Read Galatian 3:4 in The Message Bible. What was Paul's purpose in bringing to their remembrance the extent of their suffering? _____

17. When someone is receptive to the Lord "by the hearing of faith," what does this allow the Holy Spirit to do? _____

18. Will your moral striving or religiosity move the Spirit of God? _____

19. Is it your power or your trust in Jesus that will expand the kingdom of God? _____

20. Read Galatians 3:5. So since our actions don't move God, does this mean that faith does?

21. Read Mark 11:22-23. What does faith move, according to these verses?

22. What was accounted to Abraham for righteousness?
    a. Arduous labor.
    b. Utter moral integrity.
    c. Belief in God.

23. Read Galatians 3:6. From this verse, how does Paul answer the question he asked in verse 5? _____

24. If righteousness was accounted to Abraham by faith, does that mean he had to earn it? _____

25. Read Romans 4:6. Complete the sentence – "God imputes righteousness _____ from our works."

26. What must you have to be a "child of Abraham"? _____

27. Read Galatians 3:7 and Romans 2:28-29. What distinguishes a real Jew from the religious ones? _____

28. Where does circumcision take place in a true believer? _____

29. A "true Jew" receives his praise from whom? _____

30. From whom do you seek your praise? _____

31. Read Galatians 3:7, Matthew 3:7-9, John 8:37-44, and Romans 9:6-8. What are these verses making clear? _____

32. Read Galatians 3:8. Through what did the Lord speak of the justification of the Gentiles?

33. To whom was it first preached? _____

34. How does God justify the heathen? _____

35. In Abraham we are all _____

36. Read Ephesians 1:3-5. How had God blessed you? _____
_____

37. Read Galatians 3:9 and Ephesians 1:3. What does it mean to you to be blessed with every spiritual blessing in heavenly places in Christ Jesus? _____

38. Read Galatians 3:9, Romans 3:27, Romans 4:2, and 1 Corinthians 1:31. Even though we as believers are blessed, does that mean we should boast? _____ Why or why not?
_____

39. Read Galatians 3:10. Reference Commentary notes. Define Curse:
_____

40. Did the Law…
    a. Help the Jews from falling into the curse.
    b. Bring on the curse and God's wrath.

41. Read Galatians 3:10. Why are those who are of the works of the Law cursed?

42. How much of the Law would a person have to obey to not be cursed? _____

43. Is it possible for man to obey all the Law? _____

44. Read Galatians 3:11 and Matthew 19:25-26 and write it out. _____
_____

45. Read Habakkuk 2:4. What is amiss with the soul of the proud? _____

46. How are the justified to live? _____

47. What is the deception in believing you can be justified by the Law (works righteousness)?
_____

48. How does a person live in right-relationship with God? (The Message) _____
   _____

49. Read Galatians 3:12. Is the Law of faith? _____

50. If faith is reliance upon Christ to save you, then what is the Law? _____
   _____

51. How prideful is it to believe you can save yourself? _____

52. Read Galatians 3:13 in the Living Bible. How does is the Law described?
   _____

53. What are you if you try to live by that "impossible system"? _____

54. What did Jesus do for the doomed living under the law?
   KJV - _____

   TCNT - _____

   LB - _____

55. What did Jesus become on our behalf and at the same time dissolve? _____

56. If Christ's only purpose in going to the cross was to redeem us from the curse, can you see what an insult it is to the Lord to continue in the Law? _____

57. Read Galatians 3:14. What made it possible for you to now receive the blessing of Abraham? _____

58. How did Abraham receive the promise? _____

59. What is the promise? _____

60. How is the blessing made manifest to us? (See Commentary notes).
   A. _____
   B. _____

61. Read Galatians 3:15. Paul gives this spiritual application to this in the following verses. How does Paul compare this spiritual principle with a natural example? _____
   _____

62. If a man's contract with another man is binding, how much more is God's contract with man binding? _____

63. Read Hebrews 6:13-18. In God's covenant with Abraham, by whom did He swear?
   _____

64. If man swears by God as a confirmation of their oath, how much more binding is God swearing by Himself? _____

65. Can God lie? _____

66. What kind of consolation are we to have in the promises of God? _____

67. Did Abraham receive the promise? _____

68. Did God keep His word? _____

69. Can we expect the same for us today? _____

70. Read Galatians 3:16. To whom were the promises made? _____

71. Who is Abraham's Seed? _____

72. Since the promise was made to only One descendant, Jesus, how is it that you are able to participate in this promise? _____

73. Read Romans 4:13-14. Through what principle was Abraham's promise established and put into effect today? _____

74. Read Galatians 3:17. How many years after God covenanted with Abraham was the Law established? _____

75. Did the Law have any effect on the promise? _____

76. If your inheritance was of the Law, what would that do to the promise? _____

77. Read Galatians 3:19. If the promise was better, even from the beginning, what was the purpose of the Law?
SE - _____

LB - _____

78. Read Romans 3:20b. How is it that we know sin? _____

79. Read Romans 7:7. Is the Law sin? _____

80. Why did the Law not make the promise of none effect? _____

81. Read Galatians 3:18 and Romans 4:13-14. What is the promise based on, that we might receive it. _____

82. How long was the law to stay in effect? _____

83. How was the Law given (LB)? _____
_____

84. Read Galatians 3:20 and 1 Timothy 2:5. Since Jesus is the Mediator between God and man, does that mean Jesus and God are not the same? _____

85. Why doesn't this mean that Jesus and God are not the same? _____
_____

86. Read Galatians 3:21. Is the Law against the promises of God? _____

87. Read Galatians 3:22. What was Law's purpose? _____
_____

88. Read Galatians 3:21. Was there a law that could give life and make us righteous? _____

89. Read Galatians 3:23. What did the law do for us before faith (grace) came? _____

90. Read Galatians 3:24-25. What was another purpose for the Law? Why? _____
_____

91. What happens after faith has come? _____

92. Has faith come? _____

93. Read Romans 8:2-4. What has the Spirit of life in Christ made you?
_____

94. Because the law was weak through the flesh, what did God do? _____

95. Read Galatians 3:24-25 and 1 Timothy 1:9-10. When God instituted the Law, did He make it for a righteous person? _____ Why or why not? _____
_____

96. Read Galatians 3:26. How do you become a son of God? _____

97. Read Romans 8:16-17. What does the Holy Spirit bare witness of?
_____

98. "And if children, then _____; heirs of God and _____-_____ with _____."

99. Read Galatians 3:27. What happened when you were baptized (fully submerged) in Christ?
_____
_____

100. Read 2 Corinthians 5:17. If you are in Christ, what are you? _____

101. What happened to the old things? _____

102. What has become new? _____

103. If you took a strawberry and dipped it in chocolate, what would the strawberry look like after its "baptism"? _____

104. This same principle applies with Christ. When you are "dipped in Christ," whom do you come out looking like? _____

105. Once you have been baptized in Christ, are you any more special than others who have endured the same process? _____

106. If you had a basket of strawberries and they all go the dip, would they all look essentially the same? _____

107. Write out the last part of Galatians 3, verse 28. _____

108. Read Ephesians 2:13-16. What has Christ done with the two (Jews and Gentiles)? _____

109. What has happened to the middle wall of separation? _____

110. What did Christ abolish in His flesh? _____

111. Why did He do this? _____

112. Do you belong to Christ? _____

113. Read Galatians 3:29. What are you, then, according to the promise? _____

114. Read 2 Peter 1:3. What have you been given through Christ's divine power? _____

115. Does this look like the fulfillment of His promises to His heirs? _____

Galatians 3:1-29
Discipleship Answer Key

. . . .

1. Read Galatians 3:1. Was the meaning of Christ's crucifixion and death presented clearly to the Galatians?
   Yes.

2. In Galatians 3:1, why was Paul thinking the Galatians had been bewitched?
   Because the Gospel had been presented to them with clarity and then they turned away quickly to the deceptions of the Judiazers.

3. Read Ephesians 2:8-9. What was the Gospel they first believed?
   They believed that Christ was crucified for them, and that they were made righteous apart from the law by His sacrifice.

4. Read John 8:31-32. What did Jesus say knowing the truth does for a person who abides in His Word?
   It makes them know freedom from the dominion of sin.

5. In Galatians 3:1 why was Paul baffled over what the Galatians had chosen to believe? Read Romans 8:2.
   Because they had turned from the freedom of the truth to the bondage of the law.

6. Read Galatians 3:2. How did the Galatians receive the Spirit?
   B. By faith in Christ.

7. According to Romans 10:17 how does faith come?
   Faith comes by hearing the message of the Good News or Gospel of Christ.

8. Referring to the other translations and paraphrases noted in the commentary, what are other ways to say, "made perfect by the flesh"?
   NIV - Trying to attain by human effort.
   SE - Trying to continue by your own power.
   TJB - End in outward observances what was begun in the Spirit.

9. Read Ephesians 2:8-9. How is a person saved?
   By grace through faith

10. According to Ephesians 2:8-9 is salvation a gift or do we have to earn it by our works?
    It is a gift. It is God who saved us and chose us to live a holy life. He did this not because "we deserve it, but because this was his plan long before the world began—to show his love and kindness to us through Christ Jesus" (NLT).

11. Read Romans 4:4-5. When a person is employed their wages are not a gift but earned. Can we earn righteousness by the good works that we do?
    No.

12. What does this truth about God justifying the ungodly reveal about the "getting what you deserve" theory.
    It nullifies or renders it invalid.

13. Read Galatians 2:21 and Galatians 3:4. What is the common denominator that causes what Christ did and the things the Galatians suffered when they first believed to be in vain?
    Trying to be justified by the works of the Law

14. Read Galatians 3:4. Why is it true that the suffering the Galatians endured for standing up for the true Gospel would be in vain?
    Because seeking to keep the Law nullifies the hearing of faith.

15. Read Galatians 3:4. If you have endured persecution for the sake of the Gospel and then compromised the Word of God, what becomes of the good that was done prior?
    It's all in vain.

16. Read Galatian 3:4 in The Message Bible. What was Paul's purpose in bringing to their remembrance the extent of their suffering?
    To encourage them not throw away or despise the learning process they have already been through.

17. When someone is receptive to the Lord "by the hearing of faith," what does this allow the Holy Spirit to do?
    To work miracles among those who believe.

18. Will your moral striving or religiosity move the Spirit of God?
    No.

19. Is it your power or your trust in Jesus that will expand the kingdom of God?
    In trusting Jesus.

20. Read Galatians 3:5. So since our actions don't move God, does this mean that faith does?
    No.

21. Read Mark 11:22-23. What does faith move, according to these verses?
    The mountain.

22. What was accounted to Abraham for righteousness?
    c. Belief in God.

23. Read Galatians 3:6. From this verse, how does Paul answer the question he asked in verse 5?
    That God worked the miracles among the Galatians by the hearing of faith.

24. If righteousness was accounted to Abraham by faith, does that mean he had to earn it?
    No.

25. Read Romans 4:6. Complete the sentence – "God imputes righteousness **apart** from our works."

26. What must you have to be a "child of Abraham"?
    Faith.

27. Read Galatians 3:7 and Romans 2:28-29. What distinguishes a real Jew from the religious ones?
    He has faith and is a Jew inwardly, from the heart.

28. Where does circumcision take place in a true believer?
    In the heart.

29. A "true Jew" receives his praise from whom?
    God.

30. From whom do you seek your praise?
    (Think about it)

31. Read Galatians 3:7, Matthew 3:7-9, John 8:37-44, and Romans 9:6-8. What are these verses making clear?
    That people, neither by the works of the Law, nor because they are descendants of Abraham, are the children of Abraham but only those who are of faith.

32. Read Galatians 3:8. Through what did the Lord speak of the justification of the Gentiles?
    He spoke of it in the Scriptures.

33. To whom was it first preached?
    To Abraham.

34. How does God justify the heathen?
    They must have faith to believe what he has done.

35. In Abraham we are all _____.
    Blessed.

36. Read Ephesians 1:3-5. How had God blessed you?
    (Think about it)

37. Read Galatians 3:9 and Ephesians 1:3. What does it mean to you to be blessed with every spiritual blessing in heavenly places in Christ Jesus?

38. Read Galatians 3:9, Romans 3:27, Romans 4:2, and 1 Corinthians 1:31. Even though we as believers are blessed, does that mean we should boast? _____ Why or why not?
   No, because we are not blessed of our own making but from trusting God. We should glory in God.

39. Read Galatians 3:10. Reference Commentary notes. Define Curse:
   A curse is that which invokes calamity of evil. It is the opposite of "blessing."

40. Did the Law...
   b. Bring on the curse and God's wrath.

41. Read Galatians 3:10. Why are those who are of the works of the Law cursed?
   Because not they or anyone can do what the Law requires, and the penalty for not doing it is to be cursed.

42. How much of the Law would a person have to obey to not be cursed?
   All of it.

43. Is it possible for man to obey all the Law?
   No.

44. Read Galatians 3:11 and Matthew 19:25-26 and write it out.
   Galatians 3:11: But that no man is justified by the law in the sight of God, it is evident: for, The just shall live by faith.
   Matthew 19:25-26: When his disciples heard it, they were exceedingly amazed, saying, Who then can be saved? But Jesus beheld them, and said unto them, With men this is impossible; but with God all things are possible.

45. Read Habakkuk 2:4. What is amiss with the soul of the proud?
   It's not upright in him.

46. How are the justified to live?
   By faith.

47. What is the deception in believing you can be justified by the Law (works righteousness)?
   That you don't need God, you can do this on your own.

48. How does a person live in right-relationship with God? (The Message)
   Live by faith in Christ.

49. Read Galatians 3:12. Is the Law of faith?
   No.

50. If faith is reliance upon Christ to save you, then what is the Law?
   Reliance upon self to save one's self.

51. How prideful is it to believe you can save yourself?
    Extremely prideful.

52. Read Galatians 3:13 in the Living Bible. How is the Law described?
    An impossible system.

53. What are you if you try to live by that "impossible system"?
    Doomed.

54. What did Jesus do for the doomed living under the law?
    KJV - He redeemed us.
    TCNT - He ransomed us.
    LB - He brought us out from under it.

55. What did Jesus become on our behalf and at the same time dissolve?
    The curse.

56. If Christ's only purpose in going to the cross was to redeem us from the curse, can you see what an insult it is to the Lord to continue in the Law?
    Yes.

57. Read Galatians 3:14. What made it possible for you to now receive the blessing of Abraham?
    Jesus dying on the cross.

58. How did Abraham receive the promise?
    By faith believing.

59. What is the promise?
    The Spirit given to us.

60. How is the blessing made manifest to us? (See Commentary notes).
    A. By our faith in Christ.
    B. By the indwelling presence of the Holy Spirit.

61. Read Galatians 3:15. Paul gives this spiritual application to this in the following verses. How does Paul compare this spiritual principle with a natural example?
    By using the example of a contract between men.

62. If a man's contract with another man is binding, how much more is God's contract with man binding?
    It is unbreakable.

63. Read Hebrews 6:13-18. In God's covenant with Abraham, by whom did He swear?
    He swore by Himself.

64.

If man swears by God as a confirmation of their oath, how much more binding is God swearing by Himself?
It cannot be broken.

65.

Can God lie?
No.

66.

What kind of consolation are we to have in the promises of God?
A strong consolation or comfort and encouragement.

67.

Did Abraham receive the promise?
Yes.

68.

Did God keep His word?
Yes.

69.

Can we expect the same for us today?
Yes.

70.

Read Galatians 3:16. To whom were the promises made?
To Abraham and his seed.

71.

Who is Abraham's Seed?
Jesus.

72.

Since the promise was made to only One descendant, Jesus, how is it that you are able to participate in this promise?
Through Christ Jesus.

73.

Read Romans 4:13-14. Through what principle was Abraham's promise established and put into effect today?
The righteousness of faith.

74.

Read Galatians 3:17. How many years after God covenanted with Abraham was the Law established?
430 years

75.

Did the Law have any effect on the promise?
No.

76.

If your inheritance was of the Law, what would that do to the promise?
It would make it of no effect.

77.

Read Galatians 3:19. If the promise was better, even from the beginning, what was the purpose of the Law?
SE - To show people the difference between right and wrong.
LB - To show men how guilty they are of breaking God's laws.

78.
> Read Romans 3:20b. How is it that we know sin?
> **By the law.**

79.
> Read Romans 7:7. Is the Law sin?
> **No.**

80.
> Why did the Law not make the promise of none effect?
> **Because it came after God made His promise to Abraham.**

81.
> Read Galatians 3:18 and Romans 4:13-14. What is the promise based on, that we might receive it?
> **Faith.**

82.
> How long was the law to stay in effect?
> **Until the coming of Christ.**

83.
> How was the Law given (LB)?
> **God gave his laws to angels to give to Moses, who then gave them to the people.**

84.
> Read Galatians 3:20 and 1 Timothy 2:5. Since Jesus is the Mediator between God and man, does that mean Jesus and God are not the same?
> **No.**

85.
> Why doesn't this mean that Jesus and God are not the same?
> **Because Galatians 3:20 is saying that Jesus is God, and God is one.**

86.
> Read Galatians 3:21. Is the Law against the promises of God?
> **No.**

87.
> Read Galatians 3:22. What was Law's purpose?
> **To make obvious that we, in ourselves, are out of right relationship with God.**

88.
> Read Galatians 3:21. Was there a law that could give life and make us righteous?
> **No.**

89.
> Read Galatians 3:23. What did the law do for us before faith (grace) came?
> **It guarded and kept us until the time of Christ and the fulfillment of the promise.**

90.
> Read Galatians 3:24-25. What was another purpose for the Law? Why?
> **To be our tutor to bring us to Christ. So that we might be justified by faith.**

91.
> What happens after faith has come?
> **We no longer need a tutor.**

92.
> Has faith come?
> **Yes.**

93.
Read Romans 8:2-4. What has the Spirit of life in Christ made you?
It has made me free from the law of sin and death.

94.
Because the law was weak through the flesh, what did God do?
He sent Jesus to be a sacrifice for sin.

95.
Read Galatians 3:24-25 and 1 Timothy 1:9-10. When God instituted the Law, did He make it for a righteous person? _____ Why or why not?
No. Because a righteous person is putting total trust, dependence, and reliance upon the Savior to be righteous, not their compliance with the Law.

96.
Read Galatians 3:26. How do you become a son of God?
Through faith in Jesus Christ.

97.
Read Romans 8:16-17. What does the Holy Spirit bare witness of?
That we are children of God.

98.
"And if children, then **heirs**; heirs of God and **joint-heirs** with **Christ**

99.
Read Galatians 3:27. What happened when you were baptized (fully submerged) in Christ?
I put on Christ.

100.
Read 2 Corinthians 5:17. If you are in Christ, what are you?
A new creature or in Christ.

101.
What happened to the old things?
They all passed away.

102.
What has become new?
All things have become new.

103.
If you took a strawberry and dipped it in chocolate, what would the strawberry look like after its "baptism"?
It would look like it was chocolate.

104.
This same principle applies with Christ. When you are "dipped in Christ," whom do you come out looking like?
Christ.

105.
Once you have been baptized in Christ, are you any more special than others who have endured the same process?
No.

106.
If you had a basket of strawberries and they were all dipped into chocolate, would they all look essentially the same?
Yes.

107. Write out the last part of Galatians 3, verse 28.
For you are all one in Christ Jesus.

108. Read Ephesians 2:13-16. What has Christ done with the two (Jews and Gentiles)?
He made them one.

109. What has happened to the middle wall of separation?
It has been broken down.

110. What did Christ abolish in His flesh?
The Jewish laws and commandments.

111. Why did He do this?
To create in Himself one new man from the two, reconciling them both to God.

112. Do you belong to Christ?

113. Read Galatians 3:29. What are you, then, according to the promise?
An heir.

114. Read 2 Peter 1:3. What have you been given through Christ's divine power?
All things that pertain to life and godliness.

115. Does this look like the fulfillment of His promises to His heirs?
Yes.

Galatians 4:1-31
Discipleship Commentary

Galatians 4:1-2

Now I say, That the heir, as long as he is a child, differeth nothing from a servant, though he be lord of all; But is under tutors and governors until the time appointed of the father. (KJV)

I am telling you this: While the heir is still a child, he is no different from a slave. It doesn't matter that the heir owns everything, because while he is a child, he must obey the people chosen to take care of him until the child reaches the age which his father set. (SE)

But remember this, that if a father dies and leaves great wealth for his little son, that child is not much better off than a slave until he grows up, even though he actually owns everything his father had. He has to do what his guardians and managers tell him to, until he reaches whatever age this father set. (LB)

Let me show you the implications of this. As long as the heir is a minor, he has no advantage over the slave. Though legally he owns the entire inheritance, he is subject to tutors and administrators until whatever date the father has set for emancipation. (TM)

(Gal. 4:1-2) Paul is now giving a human illustration to show the state of spiritual immaturity that one experiences by being under the Law. Paul states that being under the Law is no better than being a slave, whereas faith in Christ brings us into a position of a full-grown son (Gal. 3:26).

"Now I say, That the heir (of an estate), as long as he is a child (a small child that has not come to maturity), differeth nothing from a servant (a slave that worked in the Roman household), though he be lord (owner) of all;

But is under tutors (a guardian of the young child's person) and governors (a guardian of the child's property) until the time appointed of the father (under Roman law the age of maturity was determined by his father)" (Gal. 4:1-2).

Paul applies this illustration in verse 3.

Galatians 4:3
Even so we, when we were children, were in bondage under the elements of the world: (KJV)

And that is the way it was with us before Christ came. We were slaves to Jewish laws and rituals for we thought they could save us. (LB)

So we [Jewish Christians] also, when we were minors were kept like slaves under (the rules of the Hebrew ritual and subject to) the elementary teachings of a system of external observations and regulations. (AMP)

That is the way it is with us: When we were minors, we were just like slaves ordered around by simple instructions (the tutors and administrators of the world), with no say in the conduct of our own lives. (TM)

(Gal. 4:3) By being under the Law and outside of Christ we were the "young child" of verses 1-2, without really any spiritual rights. Paul states we "were in bondage under the elements of the world." These were the elementary ABCs or fundamental principles of discipline (this has special reference to the Law).

The Revised Standard Version translates this phrase, "We were slaves to the elemental spirits of the universe." If this translation were true, then Paul is referring to the demonic spirits that brought bondage to our lives before we came to Christ. All of this adds up to this: Being under the Law makes us slaves, and the Law does not have the power to free us from the flesh or the demonic realm. (In fact, it gives place to the devil because we are operating in our own strength.) Faith in Christ gives us deliverance from both.

Galatians 4:4-5
But when the fullness of the time was come, God sent forth his Son, made of a woman, made under the law, To redeem them that were under the law, that we might receive the adoption of sons. (KJV)

But when the right time came, God sent His Son. God's Son was born from a woman; he lived under law. God did this, so that He could buy back the freedom of those who were under law. God's purpose was to make us His children. (SE)

But when the time arrived that was set by God the Father, God sent his Son, born among us of a woman, born under the conditions of the law so that he might redeem those of us who have been kidnapped by the law. Thus we have been set free to experience our rightful heritage. (TM)

(Gal. 4:4-5) When the right time of God's choosing came, God sent forth His Son in His pre-existent state from heaven into the world. He was born of a woman (virgin birth) and was made subject to the requirements of the Law.

His purpose in coming into the world was two-fold:

1. To "redeem" free, and release those under Law. He did this by perfectly keeping it, fulfilling it, and paying its curse (Matt. 5:17, Gal. 3:13). Thus, Christ delivered us from the entire system of the Law. The Greek word for "redeem" used here is EX-AGORAZO and means, "to buy OUT OF the slave market." "The word law is not preceded by the definite article, hence law in general is referred to here" (*Wuest Word Studies*, Volume 1, p. 115). This system of Law was then superseded by grace with an emphasis on living by faith.

2. To give us the status of sonship with all its privileges (*USB Handbook*, p. 91). In the Greek, the expression means "adult-sons." Under grace, we are treated as adults, not babies.

Galatians 4:6

And because ye are sons, God hath sent forth the Spirit of His Son into your hearts, crying, Abba, Father. (KJV)

And because we are His sons, God has sent the Spirit of this Son into our hearts, so now we can rightly speak of God as our dear Father. (LB)

You can tell for sure that you are now fully adopted as His own children because God sent the Spirit of His Son into our lives crying out, "Papa! Father! (TM)

(Gal. 4:6) One of the benefits of being God's sons is receiving the indwelling of His Son's Spirit. This allows the believer to address God the Father in the same manner that Jesus did (Mark. 14:35-36). The word "abba" is an Aramaic word used by Jesus (Mark. 14:36) and carries the idea of God being our "Daddy." It is a term used for intimacy and affectionate fondness. It removes the idea of God as our strict judge and carries the idea of Him being a loving Father who cares, understands, and is our best friend.

Galatians 4:7

Wherefore thou art no more a servant, but a son; and if a son, then an heir of God through Christ. (KJV)

So you are no longer a slave, but a son; and since you are a son, God has made you also an heir. (NIV)

Now we are no longer slaves, but God's own sons. And since we are His sons, everything He has belongs to us, for that is the way God planned. (LB)

Doesn't that privilege of intimate conversation with God make it plain that you are not a slave, but a child? And if you are a child, you're also an heir, with complete access to the inheritance. (TM)

(Gal. 4:7) Paul States that we are no longer slaves to the Law, but adult sons in the family of God. And if a son, an heir of God (not an heir of Rockefeller but of God), receiving all that was promised to Christ.

Galatians 4:8

Howbeit then, when ye knew not God, ye did service unto them which by nature are no gods. (KJV)

Formerly, when you did not know God, you were in bondage to beings that by nature are no gods; (RSV)

Earlier, before you knew God personally, you were enslaved to so-called gods that had nothing of the divine about them. (TM)

(Gal. 4:8) Formerly, before the Galatian Christians knew God in an intimate way through Christ, they were slaves and in bondage to idols (1 Cor. 12:2). This passage may also refer to the demonic spirits behind their false religion. In reality, although called gods, there is only one true God by nature, i.e., one divine Spirit, which is God. Those objects, which the Galatians formerly worshiped and were subject to, were really no gods at all. "Just as Paul had pointed out to Peter that they were Jews "naturally," so here he points out that, by the very nature of the case, these "elements" could not be gods...To Paul, the great sin of idolatry is to worship the created thing rather than the creator (Rom. 1:5); and whether it be the "elements" or the "heavenly bodies," all are the work of Gods' hand" (TNCT, p. 118).

Galatians 4:9-11

But now, after that ye have known God, or rather are known of God, how turn ye again to the weak and beggarly elements, whereunto ye desire again to be in bondage? Ye observe days, and months, and times, and years. I am afraid for you, lest I have bestowed upon you labour in vain. (KJV)

Now however that you have come to be acquainted with and understand and know [the true] God, or rather to be understood and known by God, how can you turn back again to the weak and beggarly and worthless elementary things [of all religions before Christ came] whose slaves you once more want to become? You observe [particular] days, and months, and seasons and years! I am alarmed [about you] lest I have labored among and over you to no purpose and in vain. (AMP)

And now that you have found God (or should I say, now that God has found you) how can it be that you want to go back again and become slaves once more to another poor, weak, useless religion of trying to get to heaven by obeying God's laws? You are trying to find favor with God by what you do or don't do on certain days or months or seasons or years. I fear for you. I am afraid that all my hard work for you was worth nothing. (LB)

But now that you know the real God – or rather since God knows you– how can you possibly subject yourselves again to those paper tigers? For that is exactly what you do when you are intimidated into scrupulously observing all the traditions, taboos, and superstitions associated with special days and seasons and years. I am afraid that all my hard work among you has gone up in a puff of smoke! (TM)

(Gal. 4:9-11) The "weak and beggarly elements" are the principles of the world's religious system that try to gain God's acceptance through various religious observances, such as observing days, months, times, and years, etc.

This is a reference back to verse 3, which speaks of the fundamental principles of a discipline (a special reference to the Law). Paul describes the "weak and beggarly elements." "WEAK" means "POWERLESS to save," and "BEGGARLY" means "POVERTY, i.e. a totally inadequate religious system, also translated worthless and beggarly (NAB, NEB).

Paul is stating, "After finding freedom through Christ Jesus, why turn back again to the bondage of trying to find God's favor and acceptance through Law? You are observing days (the Sabbath), months and times (New Moons – Num. 10:10; Passover, First fruits, etc.), years (the Sabbath Year Lev. 25:4, the Year of Jubilee, etc.)."

If the Galatians persist in turning back to the Law for their justification, Paul fears that his labor has been in vain.

Galatians 4:12

Brethren, I beseech you, be as I am; for I am as ye are: ye have not injured me at all. (KJV)

Dear brothers, please feel as I do about these things, for I am as free from these chains as you used to be. You did not despise me then when I first preached to you, (LB)

My dear friends, what I would really like you to do is try to put yourselves in my shoes to the same extent that I, when I was with you, put myself in yours. You were very sensitive and kind then. You did not come down on me personally. (TM)

(Gal. 4:12) Paul is now pleading with the Galatians. "Most likely he is exhorting the Galatians to imitate him in abandoning the law as a means of being reconciled to God. In other words, although Paul was a Jew, he has become like the Galatians, that is, as a Gentile, free from the clutches of the law. That he regarded himself as outside the law is clear from 1 Corinthians 9:20-21" (*USB Handbook*, p. 100).

Galatians 4:13-14

Ye know how through infirmity of the flesh I preached the gospel unto you at the first. And my temptation which was in my flesh ye despised not, nor rejected; but received me as an angel of God, even as Christ Jesus. (KJV)

You know it was because of a bodily ailment that I preached the gospel to you at first; And though my condition was a trial to you, you did not scorn or despise me, but received me as an angel of God, as Christ Jesus. (RSV)

You were well aware that the reason I ended up preaching to you was that I was physically broken, and so, prevented from continuing my journey, I was forced to stop with you. That is how I came to preach to you.

And don't you remember that even though taking in a sick guest was most troublesome for you, you chose to treat me as well as you would have treated an angel of God – as well as you would have treated Jesus himself if he had visited you? (TM)

(Gal. 4:13) This verse of scripure tells us that when Paul first preached the Gospel to the Galatians, he was suffering an infirmity. This was during Paul's first missionary trip to Galatia, and Galatia consisted of the Roman province that included Antioch, Iconium, Derbe, and Lystra. By going to the book of Acts, we discover in chapter 14, verses 1-22, that Paul at Lystra was dragged out of the city and stoned. Acts 14:20 tells us that as the disciples stood around him, he rose up and came into the city. The next day, he departed with Barnabas to Derbe. What do you think his appearance might have been after being stoned severely, having rocks hit him in the face and all parts of his body? Don't you imagine that his eyes might have been swollen, that his face would be black and blue? In Galatians 4:15 Paul says of these people that he's writing that if it would have been possible, many would have plucked out their own eyes and given them to him. I believe that this was a man-induced infirmity and not an illness or severe eye disease, which many theologians have projected into this passage. I believe that the book of Acts defines and instructs us as to what this infirmity of the flesh was that Paul mentioned in Galatians 4:13-14.

Galatians 4:15
Where is then the blessedness ye spake of? for I bear you record, that, if it had been possible, ye would have plucked out your own eyes, and have given them to me. (KJV)

What has happened to all your joy? I can testify that, if you could have done so, you would have torn out your own eyes and given them to replace mine if that would have helped me. (LB)

What has become of that blessed enjoyment and satisfaction and self-congratulation that once was yours [in what I taught you and your regard for me]? For I bear you witness that you would have torn out your own eyes and have given them to me [to replace mine], if that were possible. (AMP)

What has happened to the satisfaction you felt at that time? There were some of you then who, if possible, would have given your very eyes to me – that is how deeply you cared! (TM)

(Gal. 4:15) Legalism causes people to lose their joy. This is what happened to the Galatians. "Where is the blessedness you used to talk about?"
Paul is stating, "You at one time would have done anything for me, even given me your own eyes if that were needful. But now you've drawn back; it is you that has changed, not I."

Galatians 4:16

Am I therefore become your enemy, because I tell you the truth? (KJV)

And now have I become your enemy because I tell you the truth? (LB)

And now have I suddenly become your enemy simply by telling you the truth? I can't believe it. (TM)

(Gal. 4:16) Because of Paul's strong correction that the Galatians were embracing a false gospel, some might have been offended and regarded Paul as an enemy. Paul is now saying, "Does telling you the truth offend you and make me your enemy?"

Galatians 4:17

They zealously affect you, but not well; yea, they would exclude you, that ye might affect them. (KJV)

These people are zealous to win you over, but for no good. What they want is to alienate you [from us], so that you may be zealous for them. (NIV)

Those false teachers who are so anxious to win your favor are not doing it for your good. What they are trying to do is shut you off from me so that you will pay more attention to them. (LB)

Those heretical teachers go to great lengths to flatter you, but their motives are rotten. They want to shut you out of the free world of God's grace so that you will always depend on them for approval and direction, making them feel important. (TM)

(Gal. 4:17) Paul has addressed the false teachers' gospel, and now he is addressing their motives. He is stating that they are zealous, but not in a good way or purpose. Their intention is to alienate the Galatians from the true Gospel and from those who teach it so that instead of the Galatians going to Christ, they will come to them (the Judiazers).

Galatians 4:18

But it is good to be zealously affected always in a good thing, and not only when I am present with you. (KJV)

It is good for people to show interest in you, but only if their purpose is always good. This is true whether I am with you or not. (SE)

It is always a fine thing [of course] to be zealously sought after [as you are, provided that it is] for a good purpose and done by reason of purity of heart and life, and not just when I am present with you. (AMP)

It is a good thing to be ardent in doing good, but not just when I am in your presence. Can't you continue the same concern for both my person and my message when I am away from you that you had when I was with you? (TM)

(Gal. 4:18) "It is good for people to show interest in you, but only if their purpose is always good. This is true whether I am with you or not" (Simple English Translation).

Galatians 4:19

My little children, of whom I travail in birth again until Christ be formed in you. (KJV)

Oh, my children, how you are hurting me! I am once again suffering for you in the pains of a mother waiting for her child to be born – longing for the time when you will finally be filled with Christ. (LB)

My little children, again I feel pain for you, such as a mother feels when she gives birth to her child. I will feel this, until Christ is fully formed in you. (SE)

Do you know how I feel right now, and will feel until Christ's life becomes visible in your lives? Like a mother in the pain of childbirth. (TM)

(Gal. 4:19) "In another letter, Paul pictures himself as a nursing mother (1 Th. 2:7); here he speaks of himself as a mother in childbirth, suffering birth pangs for the Galatians who, by implication, are thought of as again in the womb, needing spiritual rebirth. Birth pangs are the most painful and at the same time the most rewarding experience of an expectant mother, and therefore they are an appropriate figure for the pain and suffering that Paul was undergoing because of the problems in the Galatian church" (*USB Handbook*, p. 106).

The word "AGAIN" tells us that at one time He (Christ) was clearly and abundantly evident in their experience. But now He ceased to be seen in the lives of the Galatian Christians" (*Wuest's Word Studies*, Volume 1, pp. 129-130).

What Paul is stating is that he wants to see the Galatians turn back to Christ and be developed and grow in Him again.

Galatians 4:20

I desire to be present with you now, and to change my voice; for I stand in doubt of you. (KJV)

How I wish I could be there with you right now and not have to reason with you like this, for at this distance I frankly don't know what to do. (LB)

Oh, I keep wishing that I was with you. Then I wouldn't be reduced to this blunt, letter writing language out of sheer frustration. (TM)

(Gal. 4:20) Paul's desire is to be with the Galatians. Paul does not regret the things that he has said to the Galatians but the tone in which he had to say them. If he were with them, he could approach them in a more gentle way. But since this was such a serious matter, the tone he used must be serious also.

The phrase "I stand in doubt of you" means "to be at a loss, to be disturbed" (*USB Handbook*, p. 107), or feel so helpless about the situation. Paul was like a parent feeling so concerned about his children going astray.

Galatians 4:21

Tell me, ye that desire to be under the law, do ye not hear the law? (KJV)

Tell me, you who want to be under the law, are you not aware of what the law says? (NIV)

Tell me now, you who have become so enamored with the law: Have you paid close attention to that law? (TM)

(Gal. 4:21) Paul is now using an allegory, a type of interpretation common among the rabbis. An allegory interprets scriptural events or persons as foreshadowing a deeper spiritual truth. In this passage, two women represent two covenants. One child represents a work of the flesh and the other a work of the Spirit (a promise).

If the Galatians wanted to be under the Law, Paul said, "It is necessary that you understand what the Law really says." (Here the Law refers to the whole Old Testament or the first five books of Moses known as the Pentateuch.).

Galatians 4:22
For it is written, that Abraham had two sons, the one by a bondmaid, the other by a freewoman. (KJV)

It is written that Abraham had two sons. The mother of one son was a slave woman. The mother of the other son was a free woman. (SE)

Abraham, remember, had two sons: one by the slave woman and one by the free woman. (TM)

(Gal. 4:22) Paul's statement "It is written" refers to a summary of Genesis chapters 16, 17 and 21. The story is about Abraham's two sons, Isaac and Ishmael. Ishmael was born of a slave woman, i.e., a slave of Abraham's wife, Sarah. Sarah was the mother of +Isaac, a freewoman, i.e., in contrast to a slave; she, of course, was not a slave.

Galatians 4:23
But he who was of the bondwoman was born after the flesh; but he of the freewoman was by promise. (KJV)

His son by the slave woman was born in the ordinary way; but his son y the free woman was born as the result of a promise. (NIV)

There was nothing unusual about the birth of the slave-wife's baby. But the baby of the freeborn wife was born only after God had especially promised he would come. (LB)

The son of the slave woman was born by human connivance; the son of the free woman was born by God's promise. (TM)

(Gal. 4:23) Abraham's son, born of his slave-wife, was conceived and born according to the natural process. Abraham's son, born through Sarah, was a work of God's Spirit, conceived when Abraham and Sarah were incapable of having children. He was born as the result of God's "promise" given to Abraham (Gen. 15).

Galatians 4:24-25
Which things are an allegory: for these are the two covenants; the one from the mount Sinai, which gendereth to bondage, which is Agar. For this Agar is mount Sinai in Arabia, and answereth to Jerusalem which now is, and is in bondage with her children. (KJV)

Which things are symbolic. For these are the two covenants: the one from Mount Sinai which gives birth to bondage, which is Hagar—for this Hagar is Mount Sinai in Arabia, and corresponds to Jerusalem which now is, and is in bondage with her children. (NKJV)

Now this is an allegory: these women are two covenants. One is from Mount Sinai, bearing children for slavery, she is Hagar. Now Hagar is Mount Sinai in Arabia; she corresponds to the present Jerusalem, for she is in slavery with her children. (RSV)

This true story is an example for us: The two women are like the two agreements. One agreement is on Mount Sinai. The people who are under this agreement are like slaves. The mother, named Hagar, is like that agreement. So Hagar is like Mount Sinai in Arabia. She represents the city of Jerusalem today. This city is a slave, and all of its people are slaves. (SE)

(Gal. 4:24-25) These births represent two covenants: the covenant of Abraham (grace) and the covenant from Mount Sinai (which is the Law).
Paul is saying that Hagar was a slave, and her children would also be slaves unless the father (who was a free man) cared to adopt them.
Hagar represents Mount Sinai and the childern represent the city of Jerusalem, which was enslaved to Rome. Hagar's children, being slaves, also correspond to the Jews' bondage of being under the Law or, as the Living Bible states, "the center of that system of trying to please God by trying to obey the commandments."

Galatians 4:26

But, Jerusalem which is above is free, which is the mother of us all. (KJV)

But our mother-city is the heavenly Jerusalem, and she is not a slave to Jewish laws. (LB)

In contrast to that, there is an invisible Jerusalem, a free Jerusalem, and she is our mother – this is the way of Sarah. (TM)

(Gal. 4:26) "The heavenly Jerusalem which is free…represents Sarah; and finally, grace and the faith way of salvation, for it is contrasted to the earthly Jerusalem which represents legalistic Judaism: (*Wuest's Word Studies*, Volume 1, pp. 133-134).

Galatians 4:27

For it is written, Rejoice, thou barren that bearest not; break forth and cry, thou that travailest not: for the desolate hath many more children than she which hath an husband. (KJV)

That is what Isaiah meant when he prophesied, "Now you can rejoice, O childless woman; you can shout with joy though you never before had a child. For I am going to give you many children—more children than the slave-wife has." (LB)

Remember what Isaiah wrote: "Rejoice, barren woman who bears no children, shout and cry out, woman who has no birth pangs, because the children of the barren woman now surpass the children of the chosen woman." (TM)

(Gal. 4:27) This is a quotation of Isaiah 54:1 from the Septuagint (the Greek translation of the Old Testament). "Rejoice, thou barren that bearest not; break forth and cry, thou that travailest not. The barren one here refers to Sarah. She was told of the Lord to break forth into singing and rejoicing. When? Before she had even yet become pregnant...for the desolate hath many more children than she which hath an husband. Sarah, though she was barren, rejoiced at the promise of God that she would one day produce more offspring than the one in her household who had already given birth to a son. The offspring of Sarah would last...being spiritual...throughout all eternity" (*Galatians*, by Bob Yandian, pp. 195-197).

Galatians 4:28-29

Now we, brethren, as Isaac was, are the children of promise. But as then he that was born after the flesh persecuted him that was born after the Spirit, even so it is now. (KJV)

You and I, dear brothers, are the children that God promised, just as Isaac was. And so we who are born of the Holy Spirit are persecuted now by those who want us to keep the Jewish laws, just as Isaac the child of promise was persecuted by Ishmael the slave-wife's son. (LB)

In the days of Hagar and Sarah, the child who came from faithless connivance (Ishmael) harassed the child who came – empowered by the Spirit—from the faithful promise (Isaac). Isn't it clear that the harassment you are now experiencing from the Jerusalem heretics follows that old pattern? (TM)

(Gal. 4:28-29) "Just as Isaac was conceived, not through natural means, but through the fulfillment of God's promise, so the Galatians also have become God's children, not through their own efforts, much less through natural and physical descent, but exclusively as a fulfillment of what God promised to Abraham" (*USB Handbook*, pp.115-116).

In the same way that Ishmael persecuted Isaac the child of promise (born by the power of God's Spirit), so it is now. Those that rely on the flesh (the Law) persecute those born of the Spirit (those that have been saved by grace).

There has always been and will always be only two kinds of religion: (1) Those of faith (grace) and (2) Those of works (Law).

Those of works will always continue to persecute those of grace (consider Cain and Abel – Gen. 4:3-8).

Galatians 4:30-31

Nevertheless what saith the scripture? Cast out the bondwoman and her son: for the son of the bondwoman shall not be heir with the son of the freewoman. So then, brethren, we are not children of the bondwoman, but of the free. (KJV)

But what does the Scripture say? "Throw out the slave woman and her son! The son of the free woman will receive everything that his father has, but the son of the slave woman will receive nothing.' Therefore, my brothers, we are not children of the slave woman. We are children of the free woman. (SE)

But the Scriptures say that God told Abraham to send away the slave-wife and her son, for the slave-wife's son could not inherit Abraham's home and lands along with the free woman's son. Dear brothers, we are not slave children, obligated to the Jewish laws, but children of the free woman, acceptable to God because of our faith. (LB)

There is a Scripture that tells us what to do: "Expel the slave mother with her son, for the slave son will not inherit with the free son." Isn't that conclusive? We are not children of the slave woman, but of the free woman. (TM)

(Gal. 4:30-31) Paul is now taking the Galatians back to the Scriptures. He is speaking from Genesis 21: 9-14. The main point being: Just as Hagar and Ishmael will not have any part in the inheritance of Isaac, so also those of the covenant of Law, with its legalism, shall not inherit the promise of justification which comes by faith.

We are not the children of the bondwoman (the Law) but acceptable to God through faith.

Galatians 4:1-31
Discipleship Questions

1. Read Galatians 4:1-2. If you were an heir, but still a child, would you have any advantage over the servants at this point? _____

2. Read Galatians 3:24-25. Who was the tutor? _____

3. What was the Law's purpose? _____

4. What must we have in order to no longer need the tutor? _____

5. Read Galatians 3:23. Until when were we to be kept under the Law? _____

6. Read Galatians 4:4-5. When did God send forth His Son? _____

7. "Born _____ the _____."

8. When Christ was born, was He yet above the Law? _____

9. Did the Law and its strict regulations still apply to Him? _____

10. Reference the commentary notes. What was the two-fold promise of God sending His Son into the world?
    1. _____
    2. _____

11. What three things did Christ do in order to "buy back our freedom"?
    1. _____
    2. _____
    3. _____

12. By what was the system of law superseded? _____

13. With an emphasis on what? _____

14. Is your simple faith **superior** or **inferior** to the complexity of the Law?

15. Read Galatians 4:6. What does he tell them that they are now? _____

16. Read Galatians 3:26. What is the only qualification needed to be His "son"? _____

17. What has God given to every one of His sons? _____

18. Read Galatians 4:6. What does the Holy Spirit cry out in our hearts? _____

19. Read Galatians 4:6 and Romans 8:16. What does the Holy Spirit bear witness to in our hearts? _____

20. How does your perception of God change after receiving His witness? (See commentary notes) _____
_____

21. Read Galatians 4:7. "Wherefore," what is established by knowing God is your Father? _____
_____

22. If you are a son, what else are you? _____

23. Now you are an heir of God _____ _____.

24. Read Galatians 3:16. Why must you go through Christ to receive the promise? _____

25. Read Galatians 4:7. Now as heirs then, what do we have? _____

26. How does The Message say the same thing? _____
_____

27. Is there anything that God has given to Christ that is withheld from us? _____

28. Read Galatians 4:8. Whom did you serve before knowing God? _____

29. Was there anything "divine" about the other gods? _____

30. Read 2 Corinthians 12:2. What does this verse call the objects of false gods? _____

31. Read Galatians 4:9 and John 15:16. Did you choose Christ? _____

32. For what purpose did He choose you? _____

33. Read Ephesians 1:4. When did God choose you? _____

34. Read Galatians 4:9. What is Paul's perplexity with the Galatians? _____
_____

35. How were the Galatians slipping back into bondage? _____

36. What does the Living Bible say the Galatians were trying to do by observing such days?
_____

37. According to the gospel of grace, had their favor been lost somewhere that they needed to find it? _____

38. How does the Living Bible define "useless religion"? _____

39. What was Paul's concern in Galatians 4:11? _____

40. Is Paul saying that it is wrong to observe certain days, months, times, or years of the Jewish tradition? (Romans 14:5-6 and Colossians 2:16) _____

41. What then is Paul saying? (Philippians 3:9 and Romans 10:3-4) _____

Philippians 3:17 in the Amplified Version says, "Brethren, together follow my example and observe those who live after the pattern we have set for you."

42. Why is it important to "observe" people's lives before following their example? _____

43. Read Luke 6:39. Can the blind lead the blind? _____

44. Philippians 3:18 reveals the spiritual condition of many who claimed to be walking with Christ. What is their spiritual condition? _____

45. Read Philippians 4:9. What is the expected result of learning, receiving, hearing, seeing and doing (following) a godly example? _____

46. How had Paul become like the Gentiles? (See Commentary Notes) _____

47. Read Galatians 4:13-14 and Romans 1:16. What is the Gospel of Christ? _____

48. What did Paul preach to the Galatians? _____

49. Should our outward appearances affect the Gospel preached? _____

50. Did Paul's abused state keep the Galatians from receiving the "power of God unto salvation?" _____

51. Because of the message Paul brought, how did the Galatians treat him? _____
_____

52. Read Galatians 4:13. What is this "infirmity of the flesh" that Paul was talking about?
_____

53. Read Galatians 4:15 in the Amplified Version. What ways describe the "mood" of the Galatians after being taught the true Gospel?
    a. _____
    b. _____
    c. _____

54. Read Galatians 4:15. What is Paul trying to stir up within the Galatians?
_____

55. Read Galatians 4:15. What would the Galatians have done for Paul if they could have?
_____

56. Read Galatians 4:16. What is the implied attitude of the Galatians toward Paul's rebuke?
_____

57. What should your attitude be toward those who chasten you in the Lord?
    a. Humility- Submissiveness
    b. Pride-Rebellion
    c. Apathy

58. What will the truth do for you according to John 8:32? _____

59. There is a saying that goes, "the truth may set you free, but it may make you angry!" Do you think the Galatians were experiencing the truth of this saying? _____

    In Proverbs 3:12 the Hebrew word for correct means, "chasten, convince, correct (-ion), plead, reason (together), rebuke, reprove." In Hebrews 12:5 the Greek word for chastisement means "tutorage, i.e. education or training; by implication, disciplinary correction: -- chastening, chastisement, instruction, nurture" (Strong).

60. Read Proverbs 3:12 and Revelation 3:19. Whom does the Lord chasten and rebuke?
_____

61. Read John 5:19 and John 14:10. Did Jesus come to show us what the Father would say and do? _____

62. Read John 14:9. Who did Jesus tell Phillip he could see when he looked at Him?
_____

63. If we want to know how God would correct His children we can look at the life of Jesus and see how He corrected the disciples. (Circle one)

    True or False

64. Did Jesus love His disciples enough to tell them the truth and correct them when they needed to change their actions or thinking about something? _____

65. How did Jesus chasten, discipline, and correct His disciples?
    A. In anger He pulled their beards and slapped them around.
    B. He ignored them and wouldn't tell them what was the right thing to do or say.
    C. He corrected them by telling them the truth and by being an example of what He saw and heard His Father say and do.

66. Read Galatians 4:16. Was Paul an enemy of the Galatians or did he love and care for them by warning them and telling them the truth? _____

67. Read Hebrews 12:7. How does God deal with you in His chastening? _____

68. Read 1 John 3:2 and Gal. 3:26. Are you a "son of God"? _____

69. Read Hebrews 12:11. What does godly chastening yield in the lives of those who receive?
    _____

70. Read John 15:1-3. The best and most effective means that God uses to correct, cleanse, and chasten His children is through the Word of God.

    True or False

71. Read Romans 9:30-10:2. The zeal of those attempting to bring the Galatians back under the Law was for what purpose? _____

72. Read Romans 10:1-3. This zeal that the Jews had was not according to _____.

73. Why is their zeal not according to knowledge? _____

74. Read Galatians 4:18. When is it good to be zealously affected (desire eagerly or intensely)?
    _____

75. When are you to carry out this spirit of zeal? _____

76. Why did Paul make it a point to say, "whether I am with you or not"? _____
    _____

77. Regardless of who is "watching" you, to whom are you ultimately accountable? _____

78. Read 1 Corinthians 15:57-58. Since you will always have victory through Christ, what three things are you to always do?
    1. _____
    2. _____
    3. _____

79. If you are going to "labor for the Lord" and carry on your task even when no one is watching, what must your motives be?
    a. Man-centered
    b. Christ-centered
    c. Self-centered

80. Read Galatians 4:19-20. What was the extent of Paul's commitment in seeing the Galatians restored to the fullness of Christ? _____

81. Read Galatians 4:11. What was Paul's fear for the Galatians? _____
_____

82. What was Paul willing to do to make sure he had not "labored in vain"? (Circle One)
    a. Throw up his hands in disgust and send another missionary to complete the task
    b. Whole-heartedly commit to their spiritual regeneration, regardless the pain or cost
    c. Leave them to their own destructive beliefs and let them figure it out.

83. When you are ministering to someone who may seem stiff-necked and rebellious, what is to be your commitment level in seeing him or her restored? _____

84. Does a parent abandon their children because they have gone astray? _____

85. What was Paul's only regret in writing the letter? _____

86. Read Ephesians 3:16-19. Paul's desire was to see "Christ formed" in the Galatians. How is it Christ is able to dwell in your heart? _____

87. Read Galatians 4:21. Do you think if the Galatians had fully understood the ramifications of the Law, they would have still wanted it? _____

88. What are people lacking, in regards to the Law, that keeps them in bondage to it? _____
_____

89. What does Galatians 3:10 say you are if you don't keep the whole Law? _____

90. Read Romans 10:2-4. What were the Israelites ignorant of? _____

91. Out of their ignorance, what did they seek to do? _____

92. Write out Romans 10:4. _____
_____

93. Read Galatians 4:22. How does The Message contrast the two births?
    a. One was born by _____
    b. The other was born by _____

94. If you do religious works out of human plotting and scheming, will it have eternal rewards? _____

95. Read Galatians 4:24-25. According to The Message, what do the two births represent? _____

96. What does the "way of Hagar" represent? _____
_____

97. In reference to the commentary notes for Galatians 4:25, to what does the Living Bible say Hagar's children being slaves correspond to? _____
_____

98. Read Galatians 4:26. If the "earthly Jerusalem" represents legalistic Judaism (slavery), what does the "heavenly Jerusalem represent? (See commentary notes) _____
_____

99. Read Galatians 4:27. What was the promise of God that would give her cause to rejoice? _____

100. Read Romans 4:17. What two things does God do?
     a. _____
     b. _____

101. What did God call Sarah's womb when it was dead and barren? _____

102. Was this promise fulfilled? _____

103. How are you to respond toward the promises of God, even if they seem impossible in the natural to achieve? _____

104. Read Romans 4:21. What is your assurance? _____

105. Reference the Commentary notes. Read Galatians 4:28-29. According to the *USB Handbook*, how did the Galatians become God's children? _____
_____
_____

106. What are the only two kinds of religion?
    1. _____
    2. _____

107. Who is always the persecutor? _____

108. Why do you think those who are in bondage of the Law persecute those who are free by grace? _____

109. What is to be your reaction as a born-again believer toward those who persecute you? (Hint: Matthew 5:44, Romans 12:14) _____
_____

110. Read Galatians 4:30-31. What did God command Abraham in regards to the slave woman?
    a. LB - _____
    b. KJV - _____
    c. SE - _____
    d. TM - _____

111. Did this command leave any open invitation for them to return to the house of promise? _____

112. Could the slave woman and her son expect to receive any inheritance from Abraham? _____

113. Who do the scriptures say that you are? (LB) _____

114. How are you acceptable to God? _____

115. If you are a child of inheritance, will you share your portion with the slave? _____

Galatians 4:1-31
Discipleship Answer Key

1. Read Galatians 4:1-2. If you were an heir, but still a child, would you have any advantage over the servants at this point?
   No.

2. Read Galatians 3:24-25. Who was the tutor?
   The Law.

3. What was the Law's purpose?
   To bring us to Christ, that we might be justified by faith.

4. What must we have in order to no longer need the tutor?
   Faith.

5. Read Galatians 3:23. Until when were we to be kept under the Law?
   Until faith came.

6. Read Galatians 4:4-5. When did God send forth His Son?
   When the fullness of time had come.

7. "Born **under** the **Law**."

8. When Christ was born, was He yet above the Law?
   No.

9. Did the Law and its strict regulations still apply to Him?
   Yes.

10. Reference the commentary notes. What was the two-fold promise of God sending His Son into the world?
    1. To redeem, free and release those under the Law.
    2. To give us the status of sonship with all it's privileges.

11. What three things did Christ do in order to "buy back our freedom"?
    1. He kept the Law.
    2. He fulfilled the Law.
    3. He paid its curse.

12. By what was the system of law superseded?
    Grace.

13. With an emphasis on what?
    Living by faith.

14. Is your simple faith superior or inferior to the complexity of the Law?
Superior.

15. Read Galatians 4:6. What does he tell them that they are now?
Sons.

16. Read Galatians 3:26. What is the only qualification needed to be His "son"?
Faith.

17. What has God given to every one of His sons?
The Holy Spirit.

18. Read Galatians 4:6. What does the Holy Spirit cry out in our hearts?
"Abba, Father."

19. Read Galatians 4:6 and Romans 8:16. What does the Holy Spirit bear witness to in our hearts?
That God is our Father, and we are His children.

20. How does your perception of God change after receiving His witness (See commentary notes)?
From a strict judge to a loving and understanding Father.

21. Read Galatians 4:7. "Wherefore," what is established by knowing God is your Father?
I am no longer a slave but a son.

22. If you are a son, what else are you?
An heir.

23. Now you are an heir of God _____ _____.
Through Christ.

24. Read Galatians 3:16. Why must you go through Christ to receive the promise?
Because the promise was made to only one descendant—Jesus.

25. Read Galatians 4:7. Now as heirs then, what do we have?
All that was promised to Christ.

26. How does The Message say the same thing?
We have complete access to the inheritance.

27. Is there anything that God has given to Christ that is withheld from us?
No.

28. Read Galatians 4:8. Whom did you serve before knowing God?
Myself, and other gods.

29. Was there anything "divine" about the other gods?
    No.

30. Read 2 Corinthians 12:2. What does this verse call the objects of false gods?
    Dumb idols.

31. Read Galatians 4:9 and John 15:16. Did you choose Christ?
    No, He chose me and appointed me.

32. For what purpose did He choose you?
    To go and bear fruit.

33. Read Ephesians 1:4. When did God choose you?
    Before the foundations of the world.

34. Read Galatians 4:9. What is Paul's perplexity with the Galatians?
    They had received freedom from bondage through Christ and wanted to leave that freedom and return to bondage again.

35. How were the Galatians slipping back into bondage?
    Through the observance of a certain days, months, times, and years.

36. What does the Living Bible say the Galatians were trying to do by observing such days?
    They were trying to find the favor of God.

37. According to the gospel of grace, had their favor been lost somewhere that they needed to find it?
    No.

38. How does the Living Bible define "useless religion"?
    Trying to get to heaven by observing the Law.

39. What was Paul's concern in Galatians 4:11?
    That the time he had spent ministering the truth to the Galatians was in vain and the slave master of the Law had overtaken them.

40. Is Paul saying that it is wrong to observe certain days, months, times, or years of the Jewish tradition? (Romans 14:5-6 and Colossians 2:16)
    No.

41. What then is Paul saying (Read Philippians 3:9 and Romans 10:3-4)?
    That the observance of the Law is not a requirement for right standing with God but only faith in Christ.

42. Philippians 3:17 in the Amplified Version says this, "Brethren, together follow my example and observe those who live after the pattern we have set for you."
Why is it important to "observe" people's lives before following their example?
Because what they believe may not be working for them, and they may do things more out of tradition than through grace.

43. Read Luke 6:39. Can the blind lead the blind?
No.

44. Philippians 3:18 reveals the spiritual condition of many who claimed to be walking with Christ. What is their spiritual condition?
They are enemies of the cross.

45. Read Philippians 4:9. What is the expected result of learning, receiving, hearing, seeing and doing (following) a godly example?
The God of peace will be with you.

46. How had Paul become like the Gentiles (See Commentary Notes)?
He was free from the clutches of the Law.

47. Read Galatians 4:13-14 and Romans 1:16. What is the Gospel of Christ?
It is the power of God to salvation.

48. What did Paul preach to the Galatians?
The Gospel of Christ.

49. Should our outward appearances affect the Gospel preached?
No.

50. Did Paul's abused state keep the Galatians from receiving the "power of God unto salvation?"
No.

51. Because of the message Paul brought, how did the Galatians treat him?
As an angel of God, even as Christ Jesus.

52. Read Galatians 4:13. What is this "infirmity of the flesh" that Paul was talking about?
The injuries that he had sustained while in Lystra of Galatia.

53. Read Galatians 4:15 in the Amplified Version. What ways describe the "mood" of the Galatians after being taught the true Gospel?
   a. **Blessed enjoyment.**
   b. **Satisfaction.**
   c. **Self-congratulation**

54. Read Galatians 4:15. What is Paul trying to stir up within the Galatians?
The memory of how blessed they were when they first believed.

55. Read Galatians 4:15. What would the Galatians have done for Paul if they could have?
    Given him their eyes.

56. Read Galatians 4:16. What is the implied attitude of the Galatians toward Paul's rebuke?
    They are offended and despise him.

57. What should your attitude be toward those who chasten you in the Lord?
    a. Humility- Submissiveness

58. What will the truth do for you according to John 8:32?
    Set you free.

59. There is a saying that goes, "the truth may set you free, but first it may make you angry!" Do you think the Galatians were experiencing the truth of this saying?
    Yes.

    In Proverbs 3:12 the Hebrew word for correct means, "chasten, convince, correct (-ion), plead, reason (together), rebuke, reprove." In Hebrews 12:5 the Greek word for chastisement means, "tutorage, i.e. education or training; by implication, disciplinary correction: -- chastening, chastisement, instruction, nurture" (Strong).

60. Read Proverbs 3:12 and Revelation 3:19. Whom does the Lord chasten and rebuke?
    Those He loves.

61. Read John 5:19 and John 14:10. Did Jesus come to show us what the Father would say and do?
    Yes.

62. Read John 14:9. Who did Jesus tell Phillip he could see when he looked at Him?
    The Father.

63. If we want to know how God would correct His children we can look at the life of Jesus and see how He corrected the disciples.
    True.

64. Did Jesus love His disciples enough to tell them the truth and correct them when they needed to change their thinking about something?
    Yes.

65. How did Jesus chasten, discipline, and correct His disciples?
    C. He corrected them by telling them the truth and by being an example of what He saw and heard His Father say and do.

66. Read Galatians 4:16. Was Paul an enemy of the Galatians or did he love and care for them by warning them and telling them the truth?
    He loved them.

67. Read Hebrews 12:7. How does God deal with you in His chastening?
    As a son.

68. Read 1 John 3:2. Are you a "son of God"?
    Yes.

69. Read Hebrews 12:11. What does godly chastening yield in the lives of those who receive?
    The peaceable fruit of righteousness.

70. Read John 15:1-3. The best and most effective means that God uses to correct, cleanse, and chasten His children is through the Word of God.
    True

71. Read Romans 9:30-10:2. The zeal of those attempting to bring the Galatians back under the Law was for what purpose?
    That the Galatians might follow after them and not Christ.

72. Read Romans 10:1-3. This zeal that the Jews had was not according to _____.
    Knowledge.

73. Why is their zeal not according to knowledge?
    Because they sought to establish their own righteousness, not based on faith in Jesus, but on the works of the Law.

74. Read Galatians 4:18. When is it good to be zealously affected (desire eagerly or intensely)?
    In doing good things.

75. When are you to carry out this spirit of zeal?
    At all times.

76. Why did Paul make it a point to say, "whether I am with you or not"?
    Because people will do good things when an "authority" figure is present, but will not be as responsible when there is no person physically present to be accountable to.

77. Regardless of who is "watching" you, to whom are you ultimately accountable?
    God.

78. Read 1 Corinthians 15:57-58. Since you will always have victory through Christ, what three things are you to always do?
    1. Be steadfast.
    2. Be immovable.
    3. Always abound in the work of the Lord.

79. If you are going to "labor for the Lord" and carry on your task even when no one is watching, what must your motives be?
    b. Christ-centered.

80. Read Galatians 4:19-20. What was the extent of Paul's commitment in seeing the Galatians restored to the fullness of Christ?
    He was willing to go through "child birth again" to do whatever it would take to see them restored to grace in Christ.

81. Read Galatians 4:11. What was Paul's fear for the Galatians?
    That he had labored in vain because they had missed the point.

82. What was Paul willing to do to make sure he had not "labored in vain"? (Circle One)
    b. Whole-heartedly commit to their spiritual regeneration, regardless the pain or cost.

83. When you are ministering to someone who may seem stiff-necked and rebellious, what is to be your commitment level in seeing him or her restored?
    It is to be zealous or to desire eagerly and intensely to see them restored.

84. Does a parent abandon their children because they have gone astray?
    No.

85. What was Paul's only regret in writing the letter?
    The rough manner in which he had to speak.

86. Read Ephesians 3:16-19. Paul's desire was to see "Christ formed" in the Galatians. How is it Christ is able to dwell in your heart?
    Through faith.

87. Read Galatians 4:21. Do you think if the Galatians had fully understood the ramifications of the Law, they would have still wanted it?
    No. It was bondage compared to the freedom Christ gives.

88. What are people lacking, in regards to the Law, that keeps them in bondage to it?
    Understanding.

89. What does Galatians 3:10 say you are if you don't keep the whole Law?
    Cursed.

90. Read Romans 10:2-4. What were the Israelites ignorant of?
    God's righteousness.

91. Out of their ignorance, what did they seek to do?
    To establish their own righteousness.

92. Write out Romans 10:4.
    For Christ is the end of the law for righteousness to every one that believeth.

93. Read Galatians 4:22. How does The Message Bible contrast the two births?
    a. One was born by human reasoning, thinking this was what God wanted them to do.
    b. The other was born by God's promise. What He said He would do.

94. If you do religious works out of human reasoning, plotting, and scheming, will it have eternal rewards?
    No.

95. Read Galatians 4:24-25. According to The Message, what do the two births represent?
    Two different ways of being in relationship with God.

96. What does the "way of Hagar" represent?
    A slave's life producing slaves as offspring.

97. In reference to the commentary notes for Galatians 4:25, to what does the Living Bible say Hagar's children being slaves correspond to?
    The system of trying to please God through obeying the Law.

98. Read Galatians 4:26. If the "earthly Jerusalem" represents legalistic Judaism (slavery), what does the "heavenly Jerusalem represent? (See Commentary notes)
    Freedom, grace, and salvation through faith.

99. Read Galatians 4:27. What was the promise of God gave Sarah that would cause her to rejoice?
    "The woman who could bear no children now has more than all the other women!" (NLT)

100. Read Romans 4:17. What two things does God do?
    a. He gives life to the dead.
    b. He calls those things which do not exist as though they did.

101. What did God call Sarah's womb when it was dead and barren?
    Abundant and fruitful.

102. Was this promise fulfilled?
    Yes, exceedingly.

103. How are you to respond toward the promises of God, even if they seem impossible in the natural to achieve?
    With the same faith.

104. Read Romans 4:21. What is your assurance?
That what He had promised, He was able also to perform.

105. Reference the Commentary notes. Read Galatians 4:28-29. According to the *USB Handbook*, how did the Galatians become God's children?
Exclusively as a fulfillment of what God promised Abraham.

106. What are the only two kinds of religion?
    1. Those of faith—grace.
    2. Those of works—Law.

107. Who is always the persecutor?
Those in the flesh or under the Law.

108. Why do you think those who are in bondage of the Law persecute those who are free by grace?
Jealousy—those under the Law want those who are not to suffer in the same way that they do.

109. What is to be your reaction as a born-again believer toward those who persecute you? (Hint: Matthew 5:44, Romans 12:14)
Bless them and pray for them.

110. Read Galatians 4:30-31. What did God command Abraham in regards to the slave woman?
    a. **LB - Send her away.**
    b. **KJV - Cast her out.**
    c. **SE - Throw them out.**
    d. **TM - Expel them.**

111. Did this command leave an open invitation for them to return to the house of promise?
No.

112. Could the slave woman and her son expect to receive any inheritance from Abraham?
No.

113. Who do the scriptures say that you are? (LB)
A child of the free woman.

114. How are you acceptable to God?
Through faith, trusting Him.

115. If you are a child of inheritance, will you share your portion with the slave?
No.

Galatians 5:1-26
Discipleship Commentary

....

Galatians 5:1
Stand fast therefore in the liberty wherewith Christ hath made us free, and be not entangled again with the yoke of bondage. (KJV)

It is for freedom that Christ has set us free. Stand firm, then, and do not let yourselves be burdened again by a yoke of slavery. (NIV)

So Christ has made us free. Now make sure that you stay free and don't get all tied up again in the chains of slavery to Jewish laws and ceremonies. (LB)

Christ has set us free to live a free life. So take your stand! Never again let anyone put a harness of slavery on you. (TM)

(Gal. 5:1) "Stand fast" is an expression of the Greek word STEKO [stay-ko], which means "to persevere, stand firm and to hold one's ground." Just as we must persevere to maintain our freedom and protection of the United States, so also we must stand fast in protecting our spiritual freedom.

The word "entangled" in Greek carries the idea of those being "ensnared or held in a net." The bondage that had ensnared the Galatians was the Law's demands in which they were trying to find God's favor or acceptance.

Paul was saying, "Freedom from self-justification through Law was purchased by Christ upon the cross, so don't let yourselves be burdened again."

Galatians 5:2
Behold, I Paul say unto you, that if ye be circumcised, Christ shall profit you nothing. (KJV)

Listen to me, for this is serious: if you are counting on circumcision and keeping the Jewish laws to make you right with God, then Christ cannot save you. (LB)

I am emphatic about this. The moment any one of you submits to circumcision or any other rule-keeping system, at that same moment Christ's hard-won gift of freedom is squandered. (TM)

(Gal. 5:2) "Apparently, the false teachers have put forth the claim that for the Galatians to be really Christians, they must first accept the rite of circumcision… Submission to circumcision would be to adopt the notion that one can win God's approval through some legalistic ritual or through doing what the law requires, and this would constitute a complete denial of the fact that freedom and sonship are God's gifts through Jesus Christ" (*USB Handbook*, p. 121).

The phrase "Christ shall profit you nothing" is another way of saying, "If you turn to religious Law for salvation, then you cannot benefit in any way from what Christ has done for you."

Galatians 5:3
For I testify again to every man that is circumcised, that he is a debtor to do the whole law. (KJV)

Again I declare to every man who lets himself be circumcised that he is obligated to obey the whole law. (NIV)

Again, I warn every man: if you allow yourselves to be circumcised, then you must follow the entire law. (SE)

I repeat my warning: The person who accepts the ways of circumcision trades all the advantages of the free life in Christ for the obligations of the slave life of the law. (TM)

(Gal. 5:3) "Once more I warn any man who allows himself to be circumcised that he is obliged to obey the whole law" (Gal. 5:3 TEV). "the law is a unit, and if a person puts himself under any part of it for justification, he is a debtor to the entire code with its requirements and its curse (Gal 3:10; Jas. 2:10)" (TBKC, p. 605). "Circumcision is only one part of the law, but to accept it is to obligate oneself to obey everything in the law" (*USB Handbook*, p. 121).

Galatians 5:4
Christ is become of no effect unto you, whosoever of you are justified by the law; ye are fallen from grace. (KJV)

You have been severed from Christ, you who are seeking to be justified by law; you have fallen from grace. (NASV)

If you try to be made right with God through law, then you are cut off from Christ – you have fallen from grace! (SE)

I suspect you would never intend this, but this is what happens. When you attempt to live by your own religious plans and projects,

you are cut off from Christ, you fall out of grace. (TM)

(Gal. 5:4) The New American Standard Bible states, "You have been SEVERED FROM CHRIST, you who are seeking to be justified by law; you have fallen from grace" (Gal 5:4). We all know how serious it is to have part of our body severed, such as an arm. How much more dangerous it is to be "severed from Christ." This has taken place because some have turned to the principle of Law for salvation.

The expression "you have fallen from grace," "should be understood not in the sense that grace has been take away from them, but in the sense that they have turned their backs on it…One may also say' you have put yourself in a place where God cannot be good to you, or show you His goodness'." (*USB Handbook*, p. 122) "Fallen from grace" is not speaking about the Arminian doctrine of losing salvation by one's sins, but rather of turning from the method of salvation (grace) to seeking salvation by another way.

Galatians 5:5

For we through the Spirit wait for the hope of righteousness by faith. (KJV)

But by faith we eagerly await through the Spirit the righteousness for which we hope. (NIV)

For we, by the help of the Spirit, are eagerly waiting for the fulfillment of our hope—that we may be pronounced righteous as a result of faith. (TCNT)

Meanwhile we expectantly wait for a satisfying relationship with the Spirit. (TM)

(Gal. 5:5) The hope of righteousness for which we eagerly await is the full consummation of our salvation. The Greek term for "wait" is also used several places in the New Testament for the return of Christ (Rom. 8:19, 23, 25, 1 Cor. 1:7, Phil. 3:20, and Heb. 9:28). The hope of righteousness begins now through imputed righteousness by faith and will conclude with outward glorification with the full manifestation of all that it means to have become a son of God (Rom. 8: 19-21).

Galatians 5:6

For in Jesus Christ neither circumcision availeth any thing, nor uncircumcision; but faith which worketh by love. (KJV)

When a person is in Christ Jesus, it doesn't matter whether he is circumcised or not. The only thing which is important is faith—the kind of faith which works through love. (SE)

For in Christ, neither our most conscientious religion nor disregard of religion amounts to anything. What matters is something far more interior; faith expressed in love. (TM)

(Gal. 5:6) Whether a person is circumcised or uncircumcised makes no difference in his or her relationship to God.

No amount of legalism can produce the Christian life. The Christian life is expressed by faith in God that manifests in expressions of love. Love is what sums up all that the Law demands (Rom. 13:8-10).

Justification through faith does not promote lawlessness but rather goes about to express the very righteousness that the Law demanded by faith and dependence upon the Spirit of God (Rom. 8:4).

Galatians 5:7
Ye did run well; who did hinder you that ye should not obey the truth? (KJV)

You were running the race well: who has cast a stumbling block in your way? Who has turned you aside from your obedience to the truth? (Con)

You were running superbly! Who cut in on you, deflecting you from the true course of obedience? (TM)

(Gal. 5:7) Paul describes the Christian experience as a race (1 Cor. 9:24-25, 2 Tim. 4:7, and Phil. 2:16). The Galatians had begun the race well, and then suddenly, the Judaizers had cut in on them and caused them to be hindered. Now they are attempting to finish the race no longer by faith but by legalism and self-effort.

Galatians 5:8
This persuasion cometh not of him that calleth you. (KJV)

It certainly isn't God who has done it, for He is the one who has called you to freedom in Christ. (LB)

This detour doesn't come from the One who called you into the race in the first place. (TM)

(Gal. 5:8) It certainly wasn't God who stopped them from obeying the truth.

Galatians 5:9
A little leaven leaveneth the whole lump. (KJV)

Just a little yeast makes the whole batch of dough rise. (SE)

But it takes only one wrong person among you to infect all the others. (LB)

It only takes a minute amount of yeast, you know, to permeate an entire loaf of bread. (TM)

(Gal. 5:9) Paul uses "yeast working through dough" twice in the New Testament (1 Cor. 5:6, Gal. 5:9). Usually "leaven" (yeast) symbolizes evil or sin in Scripture (Mark. 8:15, 1 Cor. 5:8). Even the smallest influence of a false gospel will eventually corrupt all, causing the whole system of grace to fall.

Galatians 5:10
I have confidence in you through the Lord, that you will be none otherwise minded: but he that troubleth you shall bear his judgment, whosoever he be. (KJV)

I am trusting the Lord to bring you back to believing as I do about these things. God will deal with that person, whoever he is, who has been troubling and confusing you. (LB)

I am confident in the Lord that you will not take a different view. The man who is unsettling you will have to pay the penalty for it, no matter who he is. (Gspd)

Deep down, the Master has given me confidence that you will not defect. But the one who is upsetting you, whoever he is, will bear the divine judgment. (TM)

(Gal. 5:10) Paul is stating that he is confident in the Lord that the Galatians will come to believe the truth concerning the Gospel of the grace of God and that the false teachers will ultimately be judged (James. 3:1), whoever they be.

Galatians 5:11
And I, brethren, if I yet preach circumcision, why do I yet suffer persecution? then is the offense of the cross ceased. (KJV)

But if I myself [as they say] still preach circumcision, why am I still persecuted? For if I preach circumcision, then the cross, the stone at which they stumble, is done away. (Con)

Some people even say that I myself am preaching that circumcision and Jewish Laws are necessary to the plan of salvation. Well, if I preached that, I would be persecuted no more—for that message doesn't offend anyone. The fact that I am still being persecuted proves that I am still preaching salvation through faith in the cross of Christ alone. (LB)

As for the rumor that I continue to preach the ways of circumcision (as I did in those pre-Damascus Road days), that is absurd. Why would I still be persecuted, then? If I were preaching that old message, no one would be offended if I mentioned the Cross now and then—it would be so watered-down it wouldn't matter one way or the other. (TM)

(Gal. 5:11) "The implication is clear that Paul at one time preached the necessity of circumcision as a means of acceptance with God" (*Wuest Word Studies*, Volume 1, p. 145). It was as a Pharisee that Paul had preached this. So if Paul was still preaching circumcision as a means of God's acceptance (the same message as the Judaizers), then why was he being persecuted by them? First Corinthians 1:23 clearly states that the preaching of Christ crucified was a stumbling block to the Jews, was an offense (v.11). Why? Because the preaching of the Gospel abolished the necessity of Law keeping as a means of acceptance with God. "That was the very point at issue when the Sanhedrin was trying Stephen. The charge was not that he was worshipping the Crucified One. It was that he was speaking blasphemous words against the Jewish temple and the Law of Moses" (Acts 6: 13-14)" (*Wuest Word Studies*, Volume 1, pp. 145-146). I'm sure that what Stephen was preaching was justification by faith apart from the Law. All of this shows the erroneous view that the first-century Jews had concerning the Law of Moses as a basis of acceptance before God.

Galatians 5:12
I would they were even cut off which trouble you. (KJV)

I wish those people who are upsetting you would add castration. (SE)

I wish those who unsettle you would mutilate themselves! (RSV)

I only wish these teachers who want you to cut yourselves by being circumcised would cut themselves off from you and leave you alone. (LB)

Why don't these agitators, obsessive as they are about circumcision, go all the way and castrate themselves? (TM)

(Gal. 5:12) Many scholars believe that Paul is referring here to the act of castration. This was a practice of priests of certain false cults that the Galatians would have been familiar with at that time.

"A possible alternative interpretation is that Paul may have had in mind the Old Testament understanding of castration which involved exclusion from God's people (Deut. 23:1)" (*USB Handbook*, pp. 129-130). This interpretation is followed by the J.B. Phillips translation, which states, "I wish those who are so eager to cut your bodies would cut themselves off from you altogether!"

Galatians 5:13

For, brethren, ye have been called unto liberty; only use not liberty for an occasion to the flesh, but by love serve one another. (KJV)

For ye, brethren, were called for freedom; only use not your freedom for an occasion to the flesh, but through love be servants one to another. (ASV)

For, dear brothers, you have been given freedom: not freedom to do wrong, but freedom to love and serve each other. (LB)

Brothers, although God called you to be free, don't use your freedom as an excuse to do all of the things which your physical body wants. Instead, serve each other through love. (SE)

It is absolutely clear that God has called you to a free life. Just make sure that you don't use this freedom as an excuse to do whatever you want to do and destroy your freedom. Rather, use your freedom to serve one another in love; that's how freedom grows. (TM)

(Gal. 5:13) Paul now "introduces a wholly new aspect of the matter of Christian liberty, the danger of abusing it. To those who have been accustomed to regarding law as the only controlling factor that stands in the way of self-indulgence and a free rein in sin, and to those who have not been accustomed to a high standard of ethics, the teaching of Christian liberty might easily mean that there is nothing to stand in the way of the unrestrained indulgence of one's own impulses. Paul often during his ministry had his hearers react in this way to his teaching of grace. The questions in Romans 6:1 and 6:15, *shall we continue in sin, that grace may abound?* And, *shall we sin because we are not under law but under grace?* were asked by someone who did not understand grace. . . . There is a recognition of the fact that the flesh is still with the Christian even though its power over him is broken, and consequently a feeling that even the child of God still needs a restraint put upon him. And this is as it should be. But the mistake that is made so often is that the Mosaic Law is substituted for the restraint of the Holy Spirit. . . ."

"The antidote against using their liberty from the law as a pretext for sinning, is found in the exhortation, 'By love serve one another.' The Greek word for LOVE here is AGAPE, which refers, not to human affection but to divine love. . . . This is a love whose chief essence is self-sacrifice for the benefit of the one who is loved... The word SERVE [in Greek] is from DOULOO which means 'to render service to, to do that which is for the advantage of someone else'" (*Wuest Word Studies*, Volume 1, pp. 148-150).

The antidote for the misuse of Christian liberty is the divine principle of love for God and love for our fellowman. As Christians, we are free to do anything as long as we can do it with perfect love for God and love for our fellowman. We are not free to do anything that we can't do with love for God and love for our fellowman.

Galatians 5:14

For all the law is fulfilled in one word, even in this; Thou shalt love thy neighbour as thyself. (KJV)

For the whole law in one utterance stands fully obeyed: namely in this, Love your neighbor as you do yourself. (Weust)

The entire law is made complete in this one command: Love other people the same way you love yourself. (SE)

For everything we know about God's Word is summed up in a single sentence: Love others as you love yourself. That's an act of true freedom. (TM)

(Gal. 5:14) Paul states in Romans 8:4 that the righteousness of the Law is to be fulfilled in the Christian by the Holy Spirit. The term "all the law" used here is not referring to the Law as a legalistic system of earning justification as Paul has been using it, but rather as the spirit of the Law as "the expression of God's will" (Rom. 7:12).

Christian love fulfills, fully performs, and fully obeys all that the Mosaic Law would require of a person. Jesus teaches the same truth under the law of Christ (Matt. 7:12, Luke 6:31-37).

The quotation that Paul is using is from Leviticus 19:18 and is applied as "love" being an eternal principle of both covenants.

The Weust's translation states, "For the whole law in one utterance stands fully obeyed: namely in this, Love your neighbor as you do yourself." Paul also speaks of this in Romans 13:8-10.

Galatians 5:15

But if ye bite and devour one another, take heed that ye be not consumed one of another. (KJV)

But if instead of showing love among yourselves you are always critical and catty, watch out! Beware of ruining each other. (LB)

Be careful! If you continue hurting each other and tearing each other apart, you might completely destroy one another. (SE)

If you bite and ravage each other, watch out—in no time at all you will be annihilating each other, and where will your precious freedom be then? (TM)

(Gal. 5:15) Paul is warning in verse 15 of what happens when the opposite of love is practiced.

A person bites with his mouth. So Paul is probably talking about the sins of malicious talk. In Classical Greek "bite, devour and consumed" all speak of the activity of wild animals destroying one another. If a person bites an apple enough times it will be consumed.

Paul's answer to these sins of the flesh is given in the following verse 16.

Galatians 5:16

This I say then, walk in the Spirit and ye shall not fulfill the lust of the flesh. (KJV)

But I say, walk and live habitually in the (Holy) Spirit—responsive to and controlled and guided by the Spirit; then you will certainly not gratify the cravings and desires of the flesh—of human nature without God. (AMP)

My counsel is this: Live freely, animated and motivated by God's Spirit. Then you won't feed the compulsions of selfishness. (TM)

(Gal. 5:16) Just as a person who is walking takes one step at a time, places one foot in front of the other, so the Christian is to take each step in his or her Christian life depending on and trusting in the Holy Spirit to deliver him from the lust of the flesh. Notice that Paul does not say that if you become strong enough as a Christian, you will not have desires of the flesh. But he says that through dependence upon the Holy Spirit, you will not fulfill the desires of the flesh. Paul states that within our natural bodies there is a Law of sin dwelling in our members (Rom. 7:20, 23). That will never change until we are glorified (1 Cor. 15:44), so we must exchange our weakness for His strength by depending upon the Holy Spirit to deliver us from sin's evil grip. This is done through faith in Christ's Spirit (Rom. 8:2, 11-13; 1 Cor. 15:57) and by yielding ourselves unto Him (Rom. 6:13).

The Holy Spirit's deliverance does not work automatically in the believer's life; He must be depended upon.

Galatians 5:17

For the flesh lusteth against the Spirit, and the Spirit against the flesh; and these are contrary the one to the other: so that ye cannot do the things that ye would. (KJV)

For the flesh lusts against the Spirit, and the Spirit against the flesh; and these are contrary to one another, so that you do not do the things that you wish. (NKJV)

The human nature wants things which are against the Spirit. The Spirit wants things, which are against our human nature. These oppose each other. Because of this, you cannot do the things that you really intend to do. (SE)

For there is a root of sinful self-interest in us that is at odds with a free spirit, just as the free spirit is incompatible with the selfishness. These two ways of life are antithetical, so that you cannot live at times one way and at times another way according to how you feel on any given day. (TM)

(Gal. 5:17-18) The flesh and the Spirit have opposite desires manifesting opposite results (Gal. 5:19-23). Paul states that this struggle causes us to not do the things that we really intend to do. A parallel passage to this would be Romans 7:19 in which Paul states, "For the good that I would I do not: but the evil which I would not that I do." Paul's answer for deliverance is not in self-effort but rather in total dependence upon the Spirit of God to break the bonds of sin by dependence upon Him (See Rom 7 and my booklet, *USDA Choice Flesh*, Don Krow).

Galatians 5:18

But if ye be led of the Spirit, ye are not under the law. (KJV)

It is by letting the Spirit lead you that you free yourselves from the yoke of the law. (Knox)

Why don't you choose to be led by the Spirit and so escape the erratic compulsions of a law-dominated existence? (TM)

(Gal. 5:18) The Galatians were still trying to live the Christian life, but were going about it by self-effort, self-dependence, and by the principle of the Law. The Spirit and the Law are contrasted and shown to be opposed to one another. The Spirit's ability to deliver from sin is quite different from the Law's ability of self-effort. Verse 18 states, "If ye be led of the Spirit, ye are not under the law," i.e., we are not under the Law's precepts in order to earn God's approval. Yielding yourself to the control of the Spirit is quite different than yielding yourself to the Law, which becomes slavery to the letter and not the Word.

Galatians 5:19-21

Now the works of the flesh are manifest, which are these; Adultery, fornication, uncleanness, lasciviousness, Idolatry, witchcraft, hatred, variance, emulations, wrath, strife, seditions, heresies, envyings, murders, drunkenness, revellings, and such like: of which I tell you before, as I have also told you in time past, that they which do such things shall not inherit the Kingdom of God. (KJV)

But when you follow your own wrong inclinations your lives will produce these evil results: impure thoughts, eagerness for lustful pleasure, idolatry, spiritism (that is, encouraging the activity of demons), hatred and fighting, jealousy and anger, constant effort to get the best for yourself, complaints and criticisms, the feeling that everyone else is wrong except those in your own little group – and there will be wrong doctrine, envy, murder, drunkenness, wild parties, and all that sort of thing. Let me tell you again as I have before, that anyone living that sort of life will not inherit the Kingdom of God. (LB)

It is obvious what kind of life develops out of trying to get your own way all the time: repetitive, loveless, cheap sex; a stinking accumulation of mental and emotional garbage; frenzied and joyless grabs for happiness; trinket gods; magic-show religion; paranoid loneliness; cutthroat competition; all-consuming-yet-never-satisfied wants; a brutal temper; an impotence to love or be loved; divided homes and divided lives; small-minded and lopsided pursuits; the vicious habit of depersonalizing every one into a rival; uncontrolled and uncontrollable addictions; ugly parodies of community. I could go on. This isn't the first time I have warned you, you know. If you use your freedom this way, you will not inherit God's Kingdom. (TM)

(Gal. 5:19-21) Paul is now giving a clearly defined standard to show whether the Holy Spirit or the flesh is leading a person. If a person is walking after the flesh he or she will manifest to some degree the works of the flesh.

Paul categorizes the works of the fleshly actions in four areas: "(1) Sensual Results: fornication, or prostitution; uncleanness, meaning moral impurity; and, lasciviousness, which deals with promiscuity such as pre-marital, extramarital, sexual relationships and things of that nature. (2) False Worship: idolatry, sorcery, and witchcraft. (3) Personal and Social Relations: enmities, meaning personal animosities; strife, meaning rivalry and discords; jealousies of an unnatural kind; wrath, people will be vengeful toward one another; factions, division within the body; divisions among individuals and within married couples; parties, envyings, meaning feelings of ill will. (4) Intemperance: drunkenness and by revellings or orgies.

Having listed all these things, he points out that people who practice these things will not enter the kingdom of God because these are works that are evidence of people who are unsaved. . . . Paul is dealing with that which is habitual practice as over against that which a believer simply falls into on an occasional basis" (*Manuscript #126*, p. 27, by Dr Arnold G. Fruchtenbaum).

The phrase "shall not inherit the kingdom of God" may be rendered in some languages as "will not enjoy having God rule over them," or "will never have the joy of God ruling them" (*USB Handbook*, p. 139).

Galatians 5:22-23

But the fruit of the Spirit is love, joy, peace, longsuffering, gentleness, goodness, faith, meekness, temperance: against such there is no law. (KJV)

But the Spirit produces love, joy, peace, patience, kindness, goodness, faithfulness, humility and self-control. There is no law against such things as these. (TEV)

But the fruit of the (Holy) Spirit, [the work which His presence within accomplishes]- is love, joy, (gladness), peace, patience (an even temper, forbearance), kindness, goodness (benevolence), faithfulness; (Meekness, humility) gentleness, self-control (self-restraint, continence). Against such things there is no law [that can bring a charge]. (AMP)

But what happens when we live God's way? He brings gifts into our lives, much the same way that fruit appears in an orchard—things like affection for others, exuberance about life, serenity. We develop a willingness to stick with things, a sense of compassion in the heart, and a conviction that a basic holiness permeates things and people. We find ourselves involved in loyal commitments, not needing to force our way in life, able to marshal and direct our energies wisely. Legalism is helpless in bringing this about; it only gets in the way. (TM)

(Gal. 5:22-23) Jesus speaks of bearing fruit in John 15 and declares, "Without me ye can do nothing," (John 15:5). Notice that this "fruit" is not produced by the believer but by the Spirit as we live in union with Him.

The Today's English Version states, "But THE SPIRIT PRODUCES, love, joy, peace, patience, kindness, goodness, faithfulness, humility, and self-control." Our part is to yield and trust; God's part is to produce the fruit.

The phrase "against such there is no law" is another way of saying "the law was never meant for people who demonstrate these qualities" or "there are no laws which speak against people who live in this way" (*USB Handbook*, p. 141).

Galatians 5:24

And they that are Christ's have crucified the flesh with the affections and lusts. (KJV)

Those who belong to Christ have nailed their natural evil desires to His cross and crucified them there. (LB)

Among those who belong to Christ, everything connected with getting our own way and mindlessly responding to what everyone else calls necessities is killed off for good—crucified. (TM)

(Gal. 5:24) "Christians crucified the evil nature with its affections and lust, in the sense that when they put their faith in the Lord Jesus…they received the actual benefits of their identification with Christ in His death on the cross" (*Wuest Word Studies*, Volume 1, p. 161). "Have crucified the flesh" is in the aorist tense suggesting an action that took place in the past. This does not refer to self-crucifixion or self-mortification but rather to Christians identifying with Christ's death. A parallel passage may be found in Romans 6:6,11, which states, "Knowing this, that our old man is crucified with him, that the body of sin might be destroyed, that henceforth we should not serve sin… Likewise reckon ye also yourselves to be dead indeed unto sin, but alive unto God through Jesus Christ our Lord."

Victory over the flesh with its passions and lusts "has been provided by Christ in His death. Faith must continually lay hold of this truth or the believer will be tempted to try to secure victory by self-effort" (TBKC, p. 609).

Galatians 5:25

If we live in the Spirit, let us also walk in the Spirit. (KJV)

If we live by the Spirit, by the Spirit let us also walk. (ASV)

If we live by the [Holy] Spirit, let us also walk by the Spirit. If by the Holy Spirit we have our life in God, let us go forward walking in line, our conduct controlled by the Spirit. (AMP)

Since we get life from the Spirit, we should follow the Spirit. (SE)

Since this is the kind of life we have chosen, the life of the Spirit, let us make sure that we do not just hold it as an idea in our heads or a sentiment in our hearts, but work out its implications in every detail of our lives. (TM)

(Gal.5:25) To "live in the Spirit" has the connotation of the Spirit being the source of our life "thus, the exhortation is to the Galatians who have divine life resident in their beings, to conduct themselves under the guidance, impulses, and energy of that life" (*Wuest Word Studies*, Volume 1, p. 162). This is twice now that Paul has admonished the Christians to walk in the Spirit (Gal. 5:16, 25).

Galatians 5:26

Let us not be desirous of vain glory, provoking one another, envying one another. (KJV)

Let us not become vainglorious and self-conceited, competitive and challenging and provoking and irritating to one another, envying and being jealous of one another. (AMP)

That means we will not compare ourselves with each other as if one of us were better and another worse. We have far more interesting things to do with our lives. Each of us is an original. (TM)

(Gal. 5:26) Paul may be expressing in a negative way the danger of failing to walk in the Spirit. What he characterizes is the manifestation of the flesh. "Vain glory may be rendered "always saying how great we are or always saying, "Look at me" (*USB Handbook*, p. 143). "Provoking one another" would be to trouble or irritate one another. "Envy" carries the idea of being jealous of one another.

Discipleship Questions
Galatians 5:1-26

1. Read Galatians 5:1. The liberty we have because Christ has made us free means:
   A. We are now free from the Law.
   B. We can live our lives in dependence upon the indwelling Holy Spirit.
   C. We are free to do what is right because it pleases the Lord and we love Him.
   D. All of the above.

2. Reference the commentary notes for Galatians 5:1. According to the definition of the word "steadfast," what is to be our attitude in this freedom? _____

3. With this fresh understanding of what it means to "stand fast" in the liberty of Jesus Christ, is there any room for acceptance or tolerance of other doctrines? _____

4. Read Galatians 2:5. What was Paul's reaction toward those who tried to subtly ensnare him back into bondage? _____

5. What is the "yoke of bondage" that is set to entangle us again? (See commentary notes) _____

6. Who is the only one responsible if you were again entangled with the yoke of bondage? _____

7. Read Colossians 2:13-14. To what were all your failures nailed? _____

8. Read Hebrews 10:10-14. Is it necessary for Christ to be re-crucified every time you sin? _____

9. Read Galatians 5:2. Define "submission to circumcision" from the commentary notes. _____

10. If you submit to "circumcision," what have you denied? _____

11. If you were to submit to "circumcision," what is the consequence to offending the cross in this manner?
    a. KJV - _____
    b. LB - _____
    c. Message - _____

12. Is God trying to "punish" you if you turn from grace back to the Law by taking away the benefits of Christ? _____ Explain _____

13. Read Galatians 5:3. What are you "trading" when you entangle yourself again in trying to fulfill the obligations of the Law? (The Message) _____

14. Read James 2:10. If you bind yourself to living by the Law, what happens if you "stumble in one point" (NKJV)? _____

15. Read Galatians 3:10. What are you if you are of the works of the Law?

16. Was circumcision the **entire issue** at hand, or just **one part** of the law used as an example?

17. Read Galatians 5:4. How serious is the consequence of getting legalistic after having come to Christ through grace? _____

18. According to the USB Handbook, is "falling from grace" the result of God pulling the rug out from under you (see commentary notes)? _____ Explain _____

19. What does The Message say you must do in order to be "cut off from Christ"? _____

20. Is there any quality of lasting fruit with man's plans apart from God? _____

"By the conviction of truth that compels us towards utter reliance upon Jesus Chris for our salvation, we eagerly await, through the help of the Spirit [helper, teacher, guide], for justification, innocence and holiness for which we have a great expectation to receive." D. Gravelle

21. Read Galatians 5:5. How is "the hope of righteousness" defined in the commentary notes?

22. Do we, as of yet, have this full consummation of righteousness? _____

23. Read 1 Timothy 4:8. When will this take place? _____

24. Have we at least begun this process? _____ How? _____

25. If we have imputed righteousness on the inside now, how will this "full consummation of righteousness" conclude (see commentary notes)? _____

26.

27. Read Galatians 5:6 and Romans 2:11. Does God show favoritism? _____
    Read Acts 10:34-35. What two things are required to be accepted by God?
    a. _____
    b. _____
28. Is this "working of righteousness" something you do to **earn favor with God** or is it what you do because you **already have favor** with Him?
29. Read Romans 10:12-13. Who shall be saved if they call upon the name of the Lord? _____
30. What example does The Message use in place of "circumcision"? _____
31. How does faith work? _____
32. Read Galatians 5:5. Through whom do we await the hope of righteousness? _____
33. What is it we must walk according to, in order to fulfill the Law? _____
34. Who is it that helps us walk in love when we really don't want to? _____
35. Could we succeed in walking in love without the Holy Spirit? _____
36. Read Galatians 13:2. What are we if we have faith without love? _____
37. Read 1 John 4:18. If we fear we are not made perfect in what? _____
38. Why do you think love dispels fear and bolsters faith?
39. Read Galatians 5:7. Did the Galatians receive the fullness of the Gospel of grace and peace at first? _____
40. What happened later? _____
41. Did they think they were still "running the race"? _____ Were they? _____
42. What is the "true race"?
    a. Obedience to the truth.
    b. Knowledge of the truth.
    c. A mixture of truth and legalism.
43. Read 1 Corinthians 9:24. If you are going to enter into a race, what is to be your goal or disposition? _____
44. Were the Galatians still **running with certainty** or in such a way as to **disqualify them-**

45. **selves?** _____
    Are there any shortcuts to be had during the true race and established course in Jesus Christ? _____

46. Read Philippians 2:16. What is the result of "holding fast the word of life"? _____

47. Read 2 Timothy 4:7. What is to be your victory cry after having run the race with all diligence and persistence? _____

48. Read Galatians 5:8. Why can't God be blamed from your turning aside from the truth? (LB) _____

49. Read Romans 16:17-18. Those who deceive the hearts of the simple with persuasive words don't serve the Lord but their own _____.

50. Read Ephesians 4:14. What is God's desire for us, according to this verse? _____

51. Read Galatians 5:9 and Matthew 16:5-12. What did Christ warn His disciples of? _____

52. What did they think He was talking about? _____

53. What is the "leaven of the Pharisees"? _____

54. Read Hebrews 13:9. What are you to not be "carried about by"? _____

55. Would this be considered "leaven" to the believer? _____

56. In what should your heart be established? _____

57. Have the "strange and various doctrines" profited those who were occupied with them? _____

58. Read Galatians 5:10. How was Paul able to have confidence in the Galatians even after they had been coerced back into legalism? _____

59. Read Galatians 5:11. What was the cause of Paul's persecution? _____

60. If Paul had been preaching "circumcision," what would have happened to the message of the cross? Con - _____

61. What is the result of watering down the Gospel? The Message - _____

62. _____

63. Read 1 Corinthians 1:22-24. What do the Jews request? _____

64. What do the Greeks seek? _____

65. What does Paul preach instead? _____

66. What is this message to the Jews and Greeks? _____

67. What is this same message to those who are called? _____

68. Does the "Rock of offense" cause people to stumble today? _____

69. Read Galatians 5:12. To what extreme was Paul taking "circumcision" to the Judaizers who were leading the Galatians astray? _____

70. What other way might this verse be interpreted? _____

71. Read Galatians 5:13. What have we been called unto? _____

72. For what does Paul warn us to not use our freedom? _____

73. How should we utilize our freedom? _____

74. What is the "chief essence of love," according the *Wuest Word Studies*, Volume 1 in the commentary notes? _____

75. What is the definition of "serve"? _____

76. What is the stipulation given as to what you can do through your Christian liberty? _____

77. Read Mark 9:35. Write out the words of Jesus. _____

Read Galatians 5:14 and 1 John 3:23. What two commandments are we to follow as New Testament believers?

78. 1. _____
    2. _____

Read Romans 13:8-10. What one commandment fulfills the entire Old Testament Law?
79. _____

80. If you truly love your neighbor, will you be committing any sins against them? _____

Read James 4:1. Where does acting evil toward each other come from?
81. _____

82. Who is the author of destruction between brethren? _____

Read Matthew 5:16. Who is supposed to receive the glory for your good works?
83. _____

Read Proverbs 18:12. What must you have to receive honor?
84. _____

Read Galatians 5:16. What does it mean to "live habitually in the Holy Spirit"?
85. _____

If you "live habitually in the Holy Spirit," what will you not gratify?
a. AMP - _____

86. b. Message - _____

In what other way is this carnality described?
87. _____

Reference the commentary notes for Galatians 5:16. Who must we depend upon for deliverance from the "flesh"?
88. _____

89. Are we able to battle this without Him? _____

What must we exchange with the Holy Spirit in order to be delivered from sin's evil grip?
90. _____

Read Romans 8:2-3, and 6-7. What has the Spirit of life in Christ done for you?
91. _____

92. Why wasn't the Law able to do this? _____

93. What is carnal mindedness? _____

Read Romans 8:6. If you do not walk in the counsel of God through the Holy Spirit, what will

94. you not have? _____

95. According to Galatians 5:16, what is the "formula" for seeing the Holy Spirit's deliverance work in your life? _____

96. Read Romans 6:12-14. What is the result of being under grace? _____

97. If sin doesn't "rule" over you any longer, what are you now able to do? (Rom. 8:1) _____

98. Read Galatians 5:17-18. What are the Spirit and the flesh to one another? _____

99. How is the flesh described in The Message? _____

100. Will you succeed in the course of life if you try to control the flesh by your own self-efforts or self-will? _____ Why not? _____

101. When the Holy Spirit delivers you, what kind of results can you expect? _____

102. When you surrender to the guidance of the Holy Spirit, what do you finally escape? The Message - _____

103. Read Galatians 5:19-20 and reference the commentary notes. What four areas categorize the "works of the flesh"?
   1. _____
   2. _____
   3. _____
   4. _____

104. How does the *USB Handbook* render "shall not inherit the Kingdom of God"? _____

105. Is Paul confronting those who simply fall into sin on an occasional basis? _____

106. Who then is he addressing? _____

107. Read Ephesians 5:1-5. "Therefore be _____ of God as dear children."

108. If you make your hearts desire to imitate God, will you be living according to the works of the flesh? _____

109. What instruction is given to us as to HOW to be imitators of God? _____

110. Verses 3-4 list more works of the flesh, but also an alternative as to how we should conduct ourselves. What is it? _____

Read Galatians 5:22-23. List the nine fruit of the Spirit.
1. _____ 6. _____
2. _____ 7. _____
3. _____ 8. _____
111. 4. _____ 9. _____
5. _____

112. If you are operating your life by walking in the Spirit, will the accuser have opportunity to convict you? _____

113. Can you produce the fruit of the Spirit by your own works, strength, or ability? _____

114. Who must you rely upon to produce the fruits of the Spirit in your life? _____

115. Can a wild branch from an apple tree decide one day that he would like to produce oranges? _____

116. What is it that determines the type of fruit a tree will produce? _____

117. Read John 15:5. Can we do anything to produce fruit apart from Christ? _____

118. What is the result of "living God's way"? (The Message) _____

119. Are the fruits of the Spirit, therefore, **GIFTS** or **GOALS** to attain?

120. Read Galatians 5:24. How is it you come to "belong to Christ"? (Gal. 3:26) _____

121. Read Galatians 2:20 and compare with Galatians 5:24. How is it that you "crucify the flesh of its affections and lusts"? _____

122. If you have been crucified with Christ, who is it that now lives in you? _____

How does the Message describe crucifying the flesh? _____

Consider your current circumstances and ask the Lord to reveal to you those areas of your life where you have responded mindlessly to what everyone else calls necessity.

123. Ask the Lord how you should prioritize your life so as to live as unto the Lord, and not unto man.

124. Read Galatians 5:25 and reference the commentary notes. How does the *Wuest Word Studies*, volume 1 p. 162 define "walking in the Spirit"? _____

125. Read Romans 12:2. To what are you not to be conformed? _____

126. If you are conformed to the world, what are you fulfilling? (Gal. 5:16) _____

127. How are you to be transformed? _____

128. If you are renewing your mind to the things of the Lord, what is at the same time being crucified? (Gal. 5:24) _____

129. What is the point of renewing your mind? _____

130. Who is it that needs to be convinced of the validity of God's word?
   a. God, because He is not sure if it really works.
   b. Our flesh/mind, because it is contrary to the Word of God.
   c. Our neighbors, because seeing is believing.

131. In comparing Romans 12:2 and Colossians 3:2, where does the real battle of crucifying the flesh take place? _____

132. How does The Message instruct us to "walk by the Spirit"? _____

133. Read Galatians 5:26. What are Paul's final instruction regarding not walking according to the flesh but to the Spirit?
   a. _____
   b. _____
   c. _____

134. What does The Message say about why we shouldn't do those things? _____

135. Consider Galatians 5:26 with the four categories of the lusts of the flesh in verses 19-21. How do they compare? _____

What does the last sentence from The Message say about you in verse 26? _____

Discipleship Answer Key
Galatians 5:1-26

....

1. Read Galatians 5:1. The liberty we have because Christ has made us free means:
   A. We are now free from the Law.
   B. We can live our lives in dependence upon the indwelling Holy Spirit.
   C. We are free to do what is right because it pleases the Lord and we love Him.
   D. All of the above.

2. Reference the commentary notes for Galatians 5:1. According to the definition of the word "steadfast," what is to be our attitude in this freedom?
   Resolute, unyielding, patient, determined.

3. With this fresh understanding of what it means to "stand fast" in the liberty of Jesus Christ, is there any room for acceptance or tolerance of other doctrines?
   No.

4. Read Galatians 2:5. What was Paul's reaction toward those who tried to subtly ensnare him back into bondage?
   He did not yield.

5. What is the "yoke of bondage" that is set to entangle us again? (See commentary notes)
   The Law's demands. Trying to find favor with God through keeping the Law.

6. Who is the only one responsible if you were again entangled with the yoke of bondage?
   Ourselves.

7. Read Colossians 2:13-14. To what were all your failures nailed?
   They were nailed to the cross.

8. Read Hebrews 10:10-14. Is it necessary for Christ to be re-crucified every time you sin?
   No.

9. Read Galatians 5:2. Define "submission to circumcision" from the commentary notes.
   To adopt the notion that one could win God's approval through some legalistic rituals or by trying to fulfill the Law.

10. If you submit to "circumcision," what have you denied?
    That freedom and sonship are God's gift through Jesus Christ.

11. If you were to submit to "circumcision," what is the consequence to offending the cross in this manner?
    a. KJV - Christ shall profit you nothing.
    b. LB - Christ cannot save you.
    c. Message - Christ's hard won gift of freedom is squandered.

12. Is God trying to "punish" you if you turn from grace back to the Law by taking away the benefits of Christ?
    No. Explain
    You cannot abide in both the Law and Christ's grace to experience freedom. Freedom comes only from the cross. You can only access the benefits by abiding in His grace.

13. Read Galatians 5:3. What are you "trading" when you entangle yourself again in trying to fulfill the obligations of the Law? (The Message)
    The advantages of the free life in Christ for the obligations of the slave life of the Law.

14. Read James 2:10. If you bind yourself to living by the Law, what happens if you "stumble in one point" (NKJV)?
    I would be guilty of the whole law.

15. Read Galatians 3:10. What are you if you are of the works of the Law?
    Cursed.

16. Was circumcision the **entire issue** at hand, or just **one part** of the law used as an example?
    It was one part of the law used as an example.

17. Read Galatians 5:4. How serious is the consequence of getting legalistic after having come to Christ through grace?
    It is very serious. Paul says you are severed from Christ, cut off, and fallen from grace because you are trying to make yourselves right with God by keeping the law.

18. According to the *USB Handbook*, is "falling from grace" the result of God pulling the rug out from under you (see commentary notes)?
    No. Explain
    It is the result of the individual turning their back on grace and positioning themselves where they cannot receive the goodness of God.

19. What does The Message say you must do in order to be "cut off from Christ"?
    Live by my own religious plans and projects.

20. Is there any quality of lasting fruit with man's plans apart from God?
    No.

"By the conviction of truth that compels us towards utter reliance upon Jesus Chris for our salvation, we eagerly await, through the help of the Spirit [helper, teacher, guide], for justification, innocence and holiness for which we have a great expectation to receive." *D. Gravelle*

21. Read Galatians 5:5. How is "the hope of righteousness" defined in the commentary notes?
    It is the full consummation of our salvation.

22. Do we, as of yet, have this full consummation of righteousness?
    No.

23. Read 1 Timothy 4:8. When will this take place?
    Upon Christ's return.

24. Have we at least begun this process?
    Yes. How?
    Through imputed righteousness by faith.

25. If we have imputed righteousness on the inside now, how will this "full consummation of righteousness" conclude (see commentary notes)?
    With the outward glorification and full manifestation of all that it means to be sons of God.

26. Read Galatians 5:6 and Romans 2:11. Does God show favoritism?
    No.

27. Read Acts 10:34-35. What two things are required to be accepted by God?
    a. Fear Him.
    b. Work righteousness (do what is right).

28. Is this "working of righteousness" something you do to **earn favor with God** or is it what you do because you **already have favor** with Him?
    I do what is right or work righteousness because I already have favor with Him.

29. Read Romans 10:12-13. Who shall be saved if they call upon the name of the Lord?
    Whosoever, anyone.

30. What example does The Message use in place of "circumcision"?
    It's either our utmost conscientiousness of religion or our disregard of it.

31. How does faith work?
    Faith works by or expresses itself in love.

32. Read Galatians 5:5. Through whom do we await the hope of righteousness?
    The Holy Spirit.

33. What is it we must walk according to, in order to fulfill the Law?
    The Holy Spirit.

34. Who is it that helps us walk in love when we really don't want to?
    The Holy Spirit.

35. Could we succeed in walking in love without the Holy Spirit?
    No.

36. Read Galatians 13:2. What are we if we have faith without love?
    We are nothing.

37. Read 1 John 4:18. If we fear we are not made perfect in what?
    Love.

38. Why do you think love dispels fear and bolsters faith?
    Because we can have faith (trust) in God when we know that He loves us.

39. Read Galatians 5:7. Did the Galatians receive the fullness of the Gospel of grace and peace at first?
    Yes.

40. What happened later?
    They were hindered by the teaching of false doctrine, which was a stumbling block.

41. Did they think they were still "running the race"?
    Yes. Were they? **No.**

42. What is the "true race"?
    a. Obedience to the truth.
    b. Knowledge of the truth.
    c. A mixture of truth and legalism.

43. Read 1 Corinthians 9:24. If you are going to enter into a race, what is to be your goal or disposition?
    To run that you may win, or obtain the prize.

44. Were the Galatians still **running with certainty** or in such a way as to **disqualify themselves**?
    They disqualified themselves.

45. Are there any shortcuts to be had during the true race and established course in Jesus Christ?
    No.

46. Read Philippians 2:16. What is the result of "holding fast the word of life"?
    To rejoice in the day of Christ, knowing that I have not run in vain.

47. Read 2 Timothy 4:7. What is to be your victory cry after having run the race with all diligence and persistence?
    I have fought the good fight, I have finished the race, I have kept the faith.

48. Read Galatians 5:8. Why can't God be blamed from your turning aside from the truth? (LB)
    Because He was the One who called me to freedom in Christ.

49. Read Romans 16:17-18. Those who deceive the hearts of the simple with persuasive words don't serve the Lord but their own _____.
Belly, or their own personal interests.

50. Read Ephesians 4:14. What is God's desire for us, according to this verse?
That we are not tossed to and fro by every wind of doctrine, by the sleight (trickery) of men, and cunning craftiness, whereby they lie in wait to deceive.

51. Read Galatians 5:9 and Matthew 16:5-12. What did Christ warn His disciples of?
The leaven of the Pharisees and Sadducees.

52. What did they think He was talking about?
Bread, because they had not brought any with them.

53. What is the "leaven of the Pharisees"?
False doctrine; legalism.

54. Read Hebrews 13:9. What are you to not be "carried about by"?
Various and strange doctrines.

55. Would this be considered "leaven" to the believer?
Yes.

56. In what should your heart be established?
Grace.

57. Have the "strange and various doctrines" profited those who were occupied with them?
No.

58. Read Galatians 5:10. How was Paul able to have confidence in the Galatians even after they had been coerced back into legalism?
He had confidence in the Lord that the true gospel of grace would still manifest in their lives.

59. Read Galatians 5:11. What was the cause of Paul's persecution?
The fact that he was preaching the Gospel of grace apart from keeping the Law.

60. If Paul had been preaching "circumcision," what would have happened to the message of the cross?
Con - It would have been done away with.

61. What is the result of watering down the Gospel?
The Message - No one is offended anymore.

62. Read 1 Corinthians 1:22-24. What do the Jews request?
A sign.

63. What do the Greeks seek?
    Wisdom.

64. What does Paul preach instead?
    Christ crucified.

65. What is this message to the Jews and Greeks?
    A stumbling stone and foolishness.

66. What is this same message to those who are called?
    The power and wisdom of God.

67. Does the "Rock of offense" cause people to stumble today?
    Yes.

68. Read Galatians 5:12. To what extreme was Paul taking "circumcision" to the Judaizers who were leading the Galatians astray?
    To the point of castration because they were so adamant about being circumcised.

69. What other way might this verse be interpreted?
    That the Judaizers would separate themselves from the Galatians and leave them alone.

70. Read Galatians 5:13. What have we been called unto?
    Freedom: liberty.

71. For what does Paul warn us to not use our freedom?
    For an occasion to the flesh to do whatever I want.

72. How should we utilize our freedom?
    To serve others in love.

73. What is the "chief essence of love," according the *Wuest Word Studies*, Volume 1 in the commentary notes?
    Self-sacrifice for the benefit of the one who is loved.

74. What is the definition of "serve"?
    To do that which is for the advantage of someone else.

75. What is the stipulation given as to what you can do through your Christian liberty?
    I can do anything as long as I can do it with perfect love for God and my fellow man.

76. Read Mark 9:35. Write out the words of Jesus.
    And he sat down, and called the twelve, and saith unto them, If any man desire to be first, the same shall be last of all, and servant of all.

77. Read Galatians 5:14 and 1 John 3:23. What two commandments are we to follow as New Testament believers?
    1. **Believe on the name of the Lord Jesus Christ.**
    2. **Love your neighbor as yourself.**

78. Read Romans 13:8-10. What one commandment fulfills the entire Old Testament Law?
    Love your neighbor as yourself.

79. If you truly love your neighbor, will you be committing any sins against them?
    No.

80. Read James 4:1. Where does acting evil toward each other come from?
    From lusts (evil and selfish desires) that war within a person.

81. Who is the author of destruction between brethren?
    The devil.

82. Read Matthew 5:16. Who is supposed to receive the glory for your good works?
    My father in heaven.

83. Read Proverbs 18:12. What must you have to receive honor?
    Humility.

84. Read Galatians 5:16. What does it mean to "live habitually in the Holy Spirit"?
    To be responsive to, and be guided and directed by the Holy Spirit.

85. If you "live habitually in the Holy Spirit," what will you not gratify?
    AMP - The cravings and desires of the flesh.
    The Message - Feed the compulsions of selfishness.

86. In what other way is this carnality described?
    Human nature without God.

87. Reference the commentary notes for Galatians 5:16. Who must we depend upon for deliverance from the "flesh"?
    The Holy Spirit.

88. Are we able to battle this without Him?
    No.

89. What must we exchange with the Holy Spirit in order to be delivered from sin's evil grip?
    Our weakness for His strength.

90. Read Romans 8:2-3, and 6-7. What has the Spirit of life in Christ done for you?
    Freed me from the law of sin and death.

91. Why wasn't the Law able to do this?
    Because it was weak through the flesh.

92. What is carnal mindedness?
    Death and enmity against God.

93. Read Romans 8:6. If you do not walk in the counsel of God through the Holy Spirit, what will you not have?
    Life and peace.

94. According to Galatians 5:16, what is the "formula" for seeing the Holy Spirit's deliverance work in your life?
    Walk and live by yielding yourself to the Holy Spirit; be responsive to and guided by Him through the Word of God.

95. Read Romans 6:12-14. What is the result of being under grace?
    Sin shall not rule me because I am no longer under the Law.

96. If sin doesn't "rule" over you any longer, what are you now able to do? (Rom. 8:1)
    Walk according to the Spirit.

97. Read Galatians 5:17-18. What are the Spirit and the flesh to one another?
    They are contrary one to another.

98. How is the flesh described in The Message?
    A root of sinful self-interest.

99. Will you succeed in the course of life if you try to control the flesh by your own self-efforts or self-will? **No.** Why not?
    Because I would be under the bondage of the Law and legalism again.

100. When the Holy Spirit delivers you, what kind of results can you expect?
     Everlasting results. Eternal redemption.

101. When you surrender to the guidance of the Holy Spirit, what do you finally escape?
     The Message - The erratic compulsions of a law-dominated existence.

102. Read Galatians 5:19-20, and reference the commentary notes. What four areas categorize the "works of the flesh"?
     1. Sensual results.
     2. False worship.
     3. Negative personal and social relationships.
     4. Intemperance.

103. How does the *USB Handbook* render "shall not inherit the Kingdom of God"?
     "Will never have the joy of God ruling them."

104. Read Galatians 5:19-21. Is Paul confronting those who simply fall into sin on an occasional basis?
No.

105. Who then is he addressing?
Those who have made the works of the flesh a habitual practice.

106. Read Ephesians 5:1-5. "Therefore be **imitators** of God as dear children."

107. If you make your hearts desire to imitate God, will you be living according to the works of the flesh?
No.

108. What instruction is given to us as to HOW to be imitators of God?
Walk in love.

109. Verses 3-4 list more works of the flesh, but also an alternative as to how we should conduct ourselves. What is it?
Always give thanks.

110. Read Galatians 5:22-23. List the nine fruit of the Spirit.
   1. **Love**
   2. **Joy**
   3. **Peace**
   4. **Patience**
   5. **Kindness**
   6. **Gentleness**
   7. **Goodness**
   8. **Faithfulness**
   9. **Self-control**

111. If you are operating your life by walking in the Spirit, will the accuser have opportunity to convict you?
No.

112. Can you produce the fruit of the Spirit by your own works, strength, or ability?
No.

113. Who must you rely upon to produce the fruits of the Spirit in your life?
The Holy Spirit.

114. Can a wild branch from an apple tree decide one day that he would like to produce oranges?
No.

115. What is it that determines the type of fruit a tree will produce?
The kind of tree that it is.

116. Read John 15:5. Can we do anything to produce fruit apart from Christ?
No.

117. What is the result of "living God's way"? (The Message)
He brings gifts into our lives.

118. Are the fruits of the Spirit, therefore, **GIFTS** or **GOALS** to attain?
Gifts.

119. Read Galatians 5:24. How is it that you come to "belong to Christ"? (Gal. 3:26)
Through faith.

120. Read Galatians 2:20 and compare with Galatians 5:24. How is it that you "crucify the flesh with its affections and lusts"?
It is through living by the faith of the Son of God. By letting Him live through you.

121. If you have been crucified with Christ, who is it that now lives in you?
Christ.

122. Read Galatians 5:24. How does the Message describe crucifying the flesh?
"Everything connected with getting our own way and mindlessly responding to what everyone else calls necessities is killed off for good—crucified."

Consider your current circumstances and ask the Lord to reveal to you those areas of your life where you have responded mindlessly to what everyone else calls necessity.

Ask the Lord how you should prioritize your life so as to live as unto the Lord, and not unto man.

123. Read Galatians 5:25 and reference the commentary notes. How does the *Wuest Word Studies*, volume 1 p. 162 define "walking in the Spirit"?
"Conducting yourself under the guidance, impulses and energy of that life."

124. Read Romans 12:2. To what are you not to be conformed?
The world.

125. If you are conformed to the world, what are you fulfilling? (Gal. 5:16)
The lusts of the flesh.

126. How are you to be transformed?
By the renewing of your mind.

127. If you are renewing your mind to the things of the Lord, what is at the same time being crucified? (Gal. 5:24)
The flesh with its passions and desires.

128. What is the point of renewing your mind?
So that we can prove to our flesh what is the good and acceptable and perfect will of God.

129. Who is it that needs to be convinced of the validity of God's word?
   a. God, because He is not sure if it really works.
   b. Our flesh/mind, because it is contrary to the Word of God.
   c. Our neighbors, because seeing is believing.

130. In comparing Romans 12:2 and Colossians 3:2, where does the real battle of crucifying the flesh take place?
   In the mind.

131. How does The Message instruct us to "walk by the Spirit"?
   "To work out its implications in every detail of our lives."

132. Read Galatians 5:26. What are Paul's final instructions regarding not walking according to the flesh but to the Spirit?
   a. Don't seek vain glory, self-conceit.
   b. Don't provoke and irritate one another.
   c. Don't be envious or jealous of one another.

133. What does The Message say about why we shouldn't do those things?
   "Because we have far more interesting things to do with our lives."

134. Consider Galatians 5:26 with the four categories of the lusts of the flesh in verses 19-21. How do they compare?
   They are the same.

135. What does the last sentence from The Message say about you in verse 26?
   "I am an original!"

Galatians 6:1-18
Discipleship Commentary

. . . .

Galatians 6:1

Brethren, if a man be overtaken in a fault, ye which are spiritual, restore such an one in the spirit of meekness; considering thyself, lest thou also be tempted. (KJV)

Dear brothers, if a Christian is overcome by some sin, you who are godly should gently and humbly help him back onto the right path, remembering that next time it might be one of you who is in the wrong. (LB)

Brothers, a person might fall into a particular sin. You people who are spiritual should repair such a person with a gentle spirit. But watch yourself! You also might be tempted to sin. (SE)

Live creatively, friends. If someone falls into sin, forgivingly restore him, saving your critical comments for yourself. You might be needing forgiveness before the day's out. (TM)

(Gal. 6:1) The word "overtaken" carries the idea of something that comes upon a person by surprise. If I were to overtake you I could hide behind a tree, and wait till you come by and then grab you. If you knew I was behind the tree I would not be able to overtake you.

Those that are walking in daily dependence upon the Spirit (the spiritual ones) are to "restore" the one that has fallen. "Restore" is used of "setting a bone that has been broken." "Meekness" means to treat in a gentle way.

This passage is not talking about getting a ball bat and hitting the one who has fallen but doing everything to restore that one back to fellowship with God and man.

Paul states also that we should consider ourselves lest we be tempted and fall.

Galatians 6:2

Bear ye one another's burdens, and so fulfill the law of Christ. (KJV)

(Share each other's troubles and problems, and so obey our Lord's command. (LB)

Help carry each other's burdens. In this way, you truly satisfy the "law" of Christ. (SE)

Stoop down and reach out to those who are oppressed. Share their burdens, and so complete Christ's law. (TM)

(Gal. 6:2) The Greek word used for "burden" here is "BAROS" [bar-os] and means "a heavy weight, burden or trouble." It is such a heavy weight that if a person is not helped in carrying it, the person will be overwhelmed. This may be either a sin (Gal. 6:1) or a circumstance of life.

As we assist in love and the helping of others we fulfill Christ's law. Our love should go beyond just not seeing someone hurt to the satisfaction of seeing him or her made happy and restored. For this is how we love ourselves (Gal. 5:14).

Galatians 6:3

For if a man think himself to be something, when he is nothing, he deceiveth himself. (KJV)

If anyone thinks he is too great to stoop to this, he is fooling himself. He is really a nobody. (LB)

If someone thinks that he is important (when he really is not), he is only fooling himself. (SE)

If you think you are too good for that, you are badly deceived. (TM)

(Gal. 6.3) "Paul wants to remind his readers that often the sight of an erring brother (v. 1) creates in some a sense of spiritual superiority rather than a genuine desire to help" (*USB Handbook*, p. 147).

We should not have an improper estimate of ourselves. To boast of our own superiority as if we could not fall into sin or fail is self-deception and results in becoming like a Pharisee.

Galatians 6:4

But let every man prove his own work, and then shall he have rejoicing in himself alone, and not in another. (KJV)

Each one should test his own actions. Then he can take pride in himself, without comparing himself to somebody else. (NIV)

Let everyone be sure that he is doing his very best, for then he will have the personal satisfaction of work well done, and won't need to compare himself with someone else. (LB)

A person should not compare himself with someone else. Each person should judge his own actions. Then he may take pride in what he himself has done. (SE)

Make a careful exploration of who you are and the work you have been given, and then sink yourself into that. Don't be impressed with yourself. Don't compare yourself with others. (TM)

(Gal. 6:4) "Something must be laid aside if a believer is to be a burden-bearer and that is conceit, an attitude that breeds tolerance of error in another and causes one to think he is above failure. The remedy for self-conceit is found in verse 4 – everyone is told to test his own actions. This means that rather than comparing himself with others he should step back and take an objective look at himself and his accomplishments (TBKC, p. 609).

The phrase "then he shall have rejoicing in himself alone" means "self-satisfaction" rather than sinful personal pride.

Galatians 6:5

For every man shall bear his own burden. (KJV)

For every man must "shoulder his own pack." (J.B. Phil)

For each one should carry his own load. (NIV)

Everyone must do his own work. (TNLT)

Each person must shoulder his own responsibility. (SE)

Each of you must take responsibility for doing the creative best you can with your own life. (TM)

(Gal. 6:5) "Here we have Paul telling us in verse 2 to bear one another's burdens but in verse 5 to bear our own burden. Is there a contradiction here? Apparently many people think so. For example, in the popular book, IS THAT IN THE BIBLE? By Dr. Charles F. Potter, there is a section on 'Contradictions.' Dr. Potter asks the question, 'In what chapter does Paul contradict himself?' The answer he gives is, 'Galatians 6.' In verse 2 Paul says 'Bear ye one another's burdens, and so fulfill the law of Christ.' In verse 5 he says 'For every man shall bear his own burden.' Unfortunately, this book (like so many other secular treatments of religious subjects) is either not quite honest or else the author did not do his homework very well. The difficulty, as you may have guessed, exists only in the English text, not in the original Greek.

"To solve this problem…we can easily see the distinctions between the two words ('burden'(s) in the Greek): In Galatians 6:2 BAROS is concerned with the burdens of temptation and weakness which come to every Christian. In 6:5 PHORTION refers to the load of work or responsibility for which each Christian must answer concerning himself. While you can help me with my infirmities, I am still responsible for my own service to the Lord and will have to make an accounting one-day (2 Cor. 5:10). At that time it will do me no good to plead, 'Well, Mr. So-and-So did less work than I did,' for we are responsible for the 'talents' (Mt. 25:14-30) and 'pounds' (Lk. 19:11-27) which the Lord gives us, not what he may give to someone else.

"It can be seen that 'burden' is not incorrect in either case, but it is certainly confusing. Some modern versions clarify the passage to a certain extent by rendering 6:2 as 'burdens' and 6:5 as 'load' (NASV and NIV). The full distinction, however, can be discovered only by using Greek study aids (such as Vine's Dictionary)." *(How to use New Testament Greek Study Aids,* by Walter Jerry Clark, pp. 99-101)

Galatians 6:6

Let him that is taught in the word communicate unto him that teacheth in all good things. (KJV)

Anyone who receives instruction in the word must share all good things with his instructor. (NIV)

Those who are taught the Word of God should help their teachers by paying them. (LB)

The man under Christian instruction should be willing to contribute toward the livelihood of his teacher. (J.B. Phil)

Be very sure now, you who have been trained to a self-sufficient maturity, that you enter into a generous common life with those who have trained you, sharing all the good things that you have and experience. (TM)

(Gal. 6:6) J. B. Phillips translates this verse in the following manner: "The man under Christian instruction should be willing to contribute toward the livelihood of his teacher." In other words, you should share all good things with those from whom you are receiving spiritual benefits.

The thought returns to bearing the burdens of others (instructor) by helping him with his ministerial work. As you help in material ways you are participating in the Lord's work by helping it continue.

"This concept of voluntary giving to provide for the Lord's servants was revolutionary since Jews were taxed for the support of their priests and Gentiles paid fees, made vows, etc., to sustain their religions" (TBKC, p. 610).

The New Testament priority of giving was: The poor, needy, and widows, as well as those who instructed others in the Word of God.

Galatians 6:7-8

Be not deceived; God is not mocked: for whatsoever a man soweth, that shall he also reap. For he that soweth to his flesh shall of the flesh reap corruption; but he that soweth to the Spirit shall of the Spirit reap life everlasting. (KJV)

Don't be fooled! You cannot mock God. A person harvests only the things which he plants. If a person lives to satisfy his human nature, then his selfish ways will bring eternal death to him. But, if a person lives to please the Spirit, he will receive eternal life from the Spirit. (SE)

Don't be misled; remember that you can't ignore God and get away with it: a man will always reap just the kind of crop he sows!
If he sows to please his own wrong desires, he will be planting seeds of evil and he will surely reap a harvest of spiritual decay and death; but if he plants the good things of the Spirit, he will reap the everlasting life which the Holy Spirit gives him. (LB)

Don't be misled: No one makes a fool of God. What a person plants, he will harvest. The person who plants selfishness, ignoring the needs of others—ignoring God!—harvests a crop of weeds. All he'll have to show for his life is weeds! But the one who plants in response to God, letting God's Spirit do the growth work in him, harvests a crop of real life, eternal life. (TM)

(Gal. 6:7-8) Paul now states, "Do not be deceived, God is not mocked!" The word "mock" in Greek literally means, "to turn up the nose at or sneer" (Thayer's Greek Lexicon). What a man plants, he will also reap as a harvest.

If a man plants his life IN THE DIRECTION OF the flesh (literally, soweth "to" the flesh), he will reap corruption (death, destruction, and will perish). But if he plants his life IN THE DIRECTION OF the Spirit, (literally "coming from or resulting from" the Spirit), he will reap life everlasting, or a harvest that will last forever.

Galatians 6:9

And let us not be weary in well doing: for in due season we shall reap, if we faint not. (KJV)

Let us not become weary in doing good, for at the proper time we will reap a harvest if we do not give up. (NIV)

So let's not allow ourselves to get fatigued doing good. At the right time we will harvest a good crop if we don't give up, or quit. (TM)

(Gal. 6:9) A parallel passage to these verses is found in Romans 2:7-9, which describes an active faith that persists until the final consummation of life eternal. Faith without works is dead, and Paul is speaking about an active faith that sows to the Spirit, manifests in well doing, and reaps everlasting life (1 John 3:7-8). The new nature and its fruit is the manifestation to the world that we belong to Him. Saving faith is not intellectual assent (James 2) As John Calvin said, " Faith alone saves but saving faith is not alone."

Galatians 6:10

As we have therefore opportunity, let us do good unto all men, especially unto them who are of the household of faith. (KJV)

Therefore, as we have opportunity, let us do good to all people, especially to those who belong to the family of believers. (NIV)

Therefore, when we have the chance to do good to anybody, we should do it, but we should give special attention to those of the household of the Faith. (SE)

So then, in like manner, let us be having opportunity, let us be working that which is good to all, but especially to those of the household of faith. (Wuest)

Right now, therefore, every time we get the chance, let us work for the benefit of all, starting with the people closest to us in the community of faith. (TM)

(Gal.6:10) The Christian's responsibility is to do good unto all men (believers and non-believers). However, there is a priority to those who are our family in the faith. In the Greek "the exhortation is not merely to do good to others when the opportunity presents itself, but to look for opportunities to do good to others" (*Wuest Word Studies*, Volume 1, p. 174).

Galatians 6:11

Ye see how large a letter I have written unto you with mine own hand. (KJV)

I am writing this myself; look at the large letters I am using! (SE)

Now, in these last sentences, I want to emphasize in the bold scrawls of my personal handwriting the immense importance of what I have written to you. (TM)

(Gal. 6:11) "Scholars believe the whole letter was written by Paul and that the big letters are a form of emphasis, similar to the modern practice of italicizing or underscoring" (*USB Handbook*, p. 154).

Galatians 6:12

As many as desire to make a fair shew in the flesh, they constrain you to be circumcised; only lest they should suffer persecution for the cross of Christ. (KJV)

Those teachers of yours who are trying to convince you to be circumcised are doing it for just one reason: so that they can be popular and avoid the persecution they would get if they admitted that the cross of Christ alone can save. (LB)

Some men are trying to force you to be circumcised. They do these things, so that the Jewish people accept them, fearing they will be persecuted, if they follow only the cross of Christ. (SE)

These people who are attempting to force the ways of circumcision on you have only one motive: they want an easy way to look good before others, lacking the courage to live by a faith that shares Christ's suffering and death. (TM)

(Gal. 6:12) The Judaizers were trying to escape persecution from their Jewish brethren who didn't believe in Christ. They maintained that if they showed the Jews that the way of salvation was still the Law, they could be accepted by them. So they were trying to force circumcision upon the church (Jews and Gentiles) as a "faith plus works" method of salvation. This would avoid the persecution that would come if they acknowledge that salvation comes only through Jesus, and Him crucified.

The Simple English Bible translates this, "Some men are trying to force you to be circumcised. They do these things, so that the Jewish people will accept them, fearing they will be persecuted, if they follow only the cross of Christ.

Galatians 6:13

For neither they themselves who are circumcised keep the law; but desire to have you circumcised, that they may glory in your flesh. (KJV)

Not even those who are circumcised obey the law, yet they want you to be circumcised that they may boast about your flesh. (NIV)

And even those teachers who submit to circumcision don't try to keep the other Jewish laws; but they want you to be circumcised in order that they can boast that you are their disciples. (LB)

All their talk about the law is gas. They themselves don't keep the law! And they are highly selective in the laws they do observe. They only want you to be circumcised so they can boast of their success in recruiting you to their side. That is contemptible! (TM)

(Gal. 6:13) Even those who have submitted to circumcision and the keeping of Law for salvation have not kept it. Even those today that insist we must keep the Law (for acceptance with God) don't keep it in its entirety. There are 613 commandments with great portions being ignored regardless of how zealous one is to keep the Law.

The Judaizers wanted the Gentiles to be circumcised so that they could boast about them becoming their disciples (members of just another Jewish sect).

Galatians 6:14

But God forbid that I should glory, save in the cross of our Lord Jesus Christ, by whom the world is crucified unto me, and I unto the world. (KJV)

As for me, God forbid that I should boast about anything except the cross of our Lord Jesus Christ. Because of the cross my interest in all the attractive things of the world was killed long ago, and the world's interest in me is also long dead. (LB)

I hope that I will never brag about something like that! The cross of our Lord Jesus Christ is my only reason for bragging. Through the cross of Jesus, my world has died to the world. (SE)

For my part, I am going to boast about nothing but the Cross of our Master, Jesus Christ. Because of that Cross, I have been crucified in relation to the world, set free from the stifling atmosphere of pleasing others and fitting into the little patterns that they dictate. (TM)

(Gal. 6:14) Even though the Judaizers boast in the works of their flesh, Paul says, "God forbid that I should boast in anything except Jesus Christ and Him crucified for me." Notice that there is a double-crucifixion. The world was crucified, and Paul was crucified unto it. This means that all of the world's system that he was involved in, including being a Pharisee, he is now dead to. Paul's meaning in life now is to live unto the risen Christ, in which he now glorifies.

Galatians 6:15
For in Christ Jesus neither circumcision availeth anything, nor uncircumcision, but a new creature. (KJV)

It doesn't make any difference now whether we have been circumcised or not; what counts is whether we really have been changed into new and different people. (LB)

It doesn't matter whether a person is circumcised or uncircumcised. All that is important is being a new creation. (SE)

Can't you see the central issue in all this? It is not what you and I do—submit to circumcision, reject circumcision. It is what God is doing, and He is creating something totally new, a free life! (TM)

(Ga. 6:15) Religious rites mean nothing. The only thing that counts is to be part of the new creation.

Galatians 6:16
And as many as walk according to this rule, peace be on them, and mercy, and upon the Israel of God. (KJV)

May God's mercy and peace be upon all of you who live by this principle and upon those everywhere who are really God's own. (LB)

All who walk by this standard are the true Israel of God – His chosen people. Peace and mercy on them! (TM)

(Gal. 6:16) Peace and mercy are available from God upon all who live according to this rule or principle of the new creation.
"The Israel of God" is probably referring to the Jewish believers.

Galatians 6:17
From henceforth let no man trouble me: for I bear in my body the marks of the Lord Jesus. (KJV)

From now on please don't argue with me about these things, for I carry on my body the scars of the whippings and wounds from Jesus' enemies that mark me as his slave. (LB)

So don't give me any more trouble. I carry the scars on my body which show that I belong to Jesus. (SE)

To conclude: Let no one give me any more trouble, because the scars I have on my body show that I am the slave of Jesus. (TEV)

Quite frankly, I don't want to be bothered anymore by these disputes. I have far more important things to do—serious living of this faith. I bear in my body scars from my service to Jesus. (TM)

(Gal. 6:17) The Today's English Version translates this verse, "To conclude: Let no one give me any more trouble, because the scars I have on my body show that I am the slave of Jesus."

Paul is referring to the practice of branding slaves in order to mark them as belonging to their master. Paul's scars were the result of his suffering and persecution for the Gospel. Paul states, "I have the marks of his ownership in my body; please don't trouble me anymore."

The book of Galatians is a heartfelt outpouring from Paul in order to get these Christians to stop walking in bondage and to walk forth in their freedom in Christ.

Galatians 6:18

Brethren, the grace of our Lord Jesus Christ be with your spirit. Amen. (KJV)

Dear brothers, may the grace of our Lord Jesus Christ be with you all. Sincerely, Paul. (LB)

May what our Master Jesus Christ gives freely be deeply and personally yours, my friends. Oh, yes! (TM)

(Gal. 6:18) Paul still acknowledged the Galatians as brothers and prays in his final words for the grace of the Lord Jesus to be with them.

Discipleship Questions
Galatians 6:1-18

Galatians 5:25-26
"Since this is the kind of life we have chosen, the life of the Spirit, let us make sure that we do not just hold it as an idea in our heads or a sentiment in our hearts, but work out its implications in every detail of our lives. That means we will not compare ourselves with one another…we have far more interesting things to do with our lives. Each of us is an original." (TM)

1. Read Galatians 6:1. When The Message says to "live creatively" it is talking about:
   A. Not being critical and negative.
   B. Not being judgemental.
   C. Walking in love.
   D. All of the above

2. What two things are you to do when someone has been "overtaken in sin"
   1. (KJV) _____
   1. (LB) _____
   1. (TM) _____
   2. (SE) _____
   2. (TM) _____
   2. (LB) _____

3. Read 1 Corinthians 15:33. Why should you consider yourself when restoring someone who is overtaken in a fault? _____

4. Read 1 Peter 4:8. What are we to have for one another above all things? _____
   Why? _____

5. Read 1 Peter 4:10. What are you to do with the gifts you have received from the Lord?
   _____

6. Read 1 Peter 4:11. Complete the sentences.
   If anyone speaks _____
   If anyone ministers _____

7. What happens when we try and minister in the flesh, or outside of our God-given abilities?
   _____

8. Is God aware of your abilities? _____

9. What is the result of allowing God to supply our abilities in ministering to our brethren? _____

10. Has God made any mistakes in supplying your abilities? _____

11. Read 2 Peter 1:3. What has God's divine power given to us? _____

12. Why is it dangerous to "compare ourselves with another" See Galatians 5:26 in light of 2 Peter 1:3? _____

13. Read Galatians 6:2-3, 1 John 3:23, and Matthew 22:37. What is the "law of Christ"? _____

14. Read Galatians 5:14. Through which command is all the Law fulfilled? _____

15. Read Galatians 6:2. How do the Living Bible and The Message describe "burdens"? _____

16. What could happen to a person who is overwhelmed with his burden, and there is no one there to help him or her carry it? _____

17. What are you if you think more highly of yourself than you should? _____

18. What reaction does the sight of an erring brother usually provoke in us? (*USB Handbook*) _____

19. What is the danger of having an improper estimate of yourself? _____

20. Read Romans 12:16. What three things are you exhorted to do?
    1. _____
    2. _____
    3. _____

21. Read Proverbs 26:12. Is a man who is wise in his own eyes truly wise? _____ Explain. _____

22. Read Galatians 6:4 and Philippians 2:12. Whose salvation are you to walk out with fear and trembling? _____

23. Can you walk out someone else's salvation for them? _____

24. What is the danger of trying to compare your walk with another's? _____

25. What is the result of self-examination? _____

26. How productive would you be if you were constantly comparing yourself and your walk with others? _____

27. What does The Message say to do after you have made a "careful exploration of who you are and the work you have been given"? _____

28. When your focus is your calling and your attitude is of humility, what is sure to be the end result? _____

29. Read Galatians 6:5. For what is each man responsible? TM - _____

30. What is the result of trying to get creative with someone else's life? _____

31. Define the two words used for "burden" from the commentary notes.
    BAROS - _____

    PHORTION - _____

32. What will you have to give account for one day? _____

33. Read 2 Corinthians 5:10. For what will we be judged at the judgment seat of Christ? _____

34. Read Galatians 6:6. What should "the man under Christian instruction be willing to contribute?
    KJV - _____

    JB Phillips - _____

    The Message - _____

35. How was this a revolutionary statement to the Jews? _____

36. What is the result of entering into a common life with your teacher? _____

37. Read 1 Corinthians 9:9-14. Was God concerned with the oxen? _____

38. With what attitude should you plow? _____

39. And if you thresh? _____

40. Is it a sin or greediness to partake of the material fruit if you have sown spiritual seeds?
_____

41. What has the Lord commanded in verse 14? _____
_____

42. What must you be careful to NOT do in this circumstance? _____
_____

43. Read Galatians 6:7-8. What are you NOT to be?
    KJV - _____

    SE - _____

    LB - _____

44. Is it possible to trick God? _____ Why not? _____
_____

45. What kind of seeds does one plant to harvest a crop of weeds and destruction? _____
_____

46. What does the Living Bible say he will reap a harvest of? _____

47. Read Romans 8:13. What is the harvest if you sow to the Spirit? _____

48. Using the list from Galatians 5:19-21, list some examples of "sowing to the flesh."
_____

49. List again the fruit of the Spirit (Galatians 5:22-23). _____
_____

50. Read Galatians 6:9. How does Paul describe an active faith? (Compare Commentary Notes and Romans 2:7)
    a. _____

    b. _____

    c. _____

51. What are we promised if we don't give up? _____

52. Read Colossians 3:17, 23-23. What is our reward for being a God-pleaser instead of a man-pleaser? _____

53. James 1:4 (AMP) – *"But let endurance and steadfastness and patience have full play and do a thorough work, so that you may be [people] perfectly and fully developed [with no defects], lacking in nothing."* What three things must you allow to have "full-play" and do a thorough work in you?
    1. _____
    2. _____
    3. _____

54. Read Galatians 6:10. Since we know that we will reap a harvest for our efforts (verse 9), what are we exhorted to do? _____

55. When is it we are "to do good unto all men"? _____

56. Although we are to do good unto all men, where should we begin our service?
_____

57. Are we to wait for opportunities to come knocking? (See Commentary Notes) _____
_____

58. Read Galatians 6:11. What was Paul trying to emphasize to the Galatians with his "bold scrawls"? _____

59. Read Galatians 6:12. Why was it the Judaizers acted deceptively in regards to the Gospel of Jesus Christ?
    LB a. _____
       b. _____
    TM a. _____
       b. _____

60. Read Galatians 2:19-20. In order to live, with Whom do you have to be crucified?
_____

61. If you are crucified with Christ, do you also share in His sufferings? _____

62. Read Galatians 6:12-13. Even though the Judaizers professed Christ with their lips, what exposed their falsity and deceitfulness? _____
_____

63. Read John 14:21 and 1 John 3:23. How can you tell if someone truly loves Christ?
_____

64. Read Galatians 6:13. Did those who were already circumcised keep the Law? _____

65. Why, then, did they require others to keep the Law through circumcision? _____
_____

66. Read Matthew 5:17 and Romans 8:3-4 (NKJV). Who was the only one who could fulfill the Law? _____

67. Read John 15:13, Romans 13:8-10, and Galatians 5:14. How was the Law fulfilled?
_____

68. Read Galatians 6:14 and Ephesians 2:8-9. Why did God save us by grace and not by our works? _____
_____

69. Read Romans 3:23-28. According to verse 23, what is man "guilty" of?
    a. _____
    b. _____

70. Read Romans 5:8. Since we couldn't save ourselves, what did God do for us? _____
_____

71. Read Romans 3:27. Where is boasting then? _____

72. Read Romans 3:28. What can we therefore conclude? _____
_____

73. Read Galatians 6:14. What is the only thing we should boast about? _____

74. From what three things does Galatians 6:14 in The Message say the cross has set us free?
    a. _____

    b. _____

    c. _____

75. Read Galatians 1:10. Can you successfully be a man-pleaser first, and a God-pleaser at the same time? _____

76. Read Galatians 6:15. What really matters in a life with Christ? (LB) _____
_____

77. Can you accomplish this by altering outside appearances? _____

78. Read Galatians 6:15. How does The Message describe what the "central issue" is?
_____
_____

79. Read 2 Corinthians 5:17. If you are in Christ, what is your true identity? _____

80. What has happened to your old identity? _____

81. Read Colossians 3:10. How can you tell if someone is a "new man"?
_____

82. Read Galatians 6:16. What will be the result if you walk out your salvation as a "new creature"? _____

83. Read Romans 9:6-7 and 2:28-29. Who are the Israel of God?
_____

84. Read Galatians 3:26, 29 and 4:28. Who are the children of the promise?
_____

85. Read Galatians 6:17. Was Paul telling the Galatians to not bother him with their troubles anymore? _____

86. Then what do you think he is talking about? _____

87. Why is it Paul is able to stand so strongly against the persecution of the Judaizers?" (SE)
_____

88. When you come to the fullness of the revelation of whom you belong, how will that change your current walk with the Lord? _____
_____

89. Read 2 Timothy 3:12. Who are they who are suffering persecution for Christ?
_____

90. Read Galatians 6:18. What is Paul's final exhortation? _____
_____

91. Why did he pray for "grace" to be upon them? _____
_____

92. How does The Message paraphrase this verse? _____
_____

Discipleship Answer Key
Galatians 6:1-18

Galatians 5:25-26
"Since this is the kind of life we have chosen, the life of the Spirit, let us make sure that we do not just hold it as an idea in our heads or a sentiment in our hearts, but work out its implications in every detail of our lives. That means we will not compare ourselves with one another...we have far more interesting things to do with our lives. Each of us is an original." (TM)

1. Read Galatians 6:1. When The Message says to "live creatively" it is talking about:
   A. Not being critical and negative.
   B. Not being judgemental.
   C. Walking in love.
   D. All of the above

2. What two things are you to do when someone has been "overtaken in sin"
   1. (KJV) Restore in the spirit of meekness.
   1. (LB) Gently and humbly help him back on the right path.
   1. (TM) Forgivingly restore him.
   2. (SE) Watch yourself—you might also be tempted.
   2. (TM) Save your critical comments for yourself.
   2. (LB) Remember that next time it might be you.

3. Read 1 Corinthians 15:33. Why should you consider yourself when restoring someone who is overtaken in a fault?
   Because evil communication (company or companionship) corrupts good manners.

4. Read 1 Peter 4:8. What are we to have for one another above all things?
   Fervent love. Why? Because love covers a multitude of sins.

5. Read 1 Peter 4:10. What are you to do with the gifts you have received from the Lord?
   Use them to minister to one another as good stewards of the manifold grace of God.

6. Read 1 Peter 4:11. Complete the sentences.
   If anyone speaks
   Let him speak as the oracles of God.
   If anyone ministers
   Let him do it with the ability God supplies.

7. What happens when we try and minister in the flesh, or outside of our God-given abilities?
   We run the risk of becoming a spiritual manipulator.

8. Is God aware of your abilities?
   Yes.

9. What is the result of allowing God to supply our abilities in ministering to our brethren?
   He is glorified through Jesus Christ.

10. Has God made any mistakes in supplying your abilities?
    No.

11. Read 2 Peter 1:3. What has God's divine power given to us?
    All things that pertain to life and godliness.

12. Why is it dangerous to "compare ourselves with another"? (See Galatians 5:26 in light of 2 Peter 1:3)
    Because when you compare your God-given abilities with someone else's and you feel yours are lacking, you are essentially saying, "God made a mistake."

13. Read Galatians 6:2-3, 1 John 3:23, and Matthew 22:37. What is the "law of Christ"?
    To love the Lord with all your heart, mind, soul, and strength. And to love your neighbor as yourself.

14. Read Galatians 5:14. Through which command is all the Law fulfilled?
    Love your neighbor as yourself.

15. Read Galatians 6:2. How do the Living Bible and The Message describe "burdens"?
    Troubles, problems, and oppression.

16. What could happen to a person who is overwhelmed with his burden, and there is no one there to help him or her carry it?
    He or she could turn back from following Christ and have a heart that is hard toward the Lord.

17. What are you if you think more highly of yourself than you should?
    Badly deceived.

18. What reaction does the sight of an erring brother usually provoke in us? (*USB Handbook*)
    A sense of spiritual superiority rather than a genuine desire to help.

19. What is the danger of having an improper estimate of yourself?
    You can become like a legalistic Pharisee, passing judgment and condemning others because you think are better than them.

20. Read Romans 12:16. What three things are you exhorted to do?
    1. **Be in unity.**
    2. **Associate with the humble.**
    3. **Don't be wise in your own opinion.**

21. Read Proverbs 26:12. Is a man who is wise in his own eyes truly wise?
    No. Explain.
    There is more hope for a fool than for him. Who in his own conceit thinks he knows everything and is not teachable.

22. Read Galatians 6:4 and Philippians 2:12. Whose salvation are you to walk out with fear and trembling?
The salvation that the Lord has given to me.

23. Can you walk out someone else's salvation for them?
No.

24. What is the danger of trying to compare your walk with another's?
You might take upon yourself the burden of walking out their salvation, which is impossible to do anyway.

25. What is the result of self-examination?
There is a temptation to get prideful and rejoice in your own accomplishments.

26. How productive would you be if you were constantly comparing yourself and your walk with others?
Your focus would not be on the Lord and you would probably not be very fruitful.

27. What does The Message say to do after you have made a "careful exploration of who you are and the work you have been given"?
"Sink yourself into that."

28. When your focus is your calling and your attitude is of humility, what is sure to be the end result?
God will use you greatly and you will have much cause for celebration.

29. Read Galatians 6:5. For what is each person responsible? (TM)
Doing his creative best with his own life.

30. What is the result of trying to get creative with someone else's life?
Bitterness and resentment.

31. Define the two words used for "burden" from the commentary notes.
BAROS - concern with the burdens of temptation and weakness of our Christian brethren.
PHORTION - personal responsibility for our own Christian work.

32. What will you have to give account for one day?
My own service to the Lord.

33. Read 2 Corinthians 5:10. For what will we be judged at the judgment seat of Christ?
The things, whether good or bad, that we have done in the body.

34. Read Galatians 6:6. What should "the man under Christian instruction" be willing to contribute?
    KJV - In all good things.
    JB Phillips - Toward the livelihood of his teacher.
    The Message - All good things that you have and experience.

35. How was this a revolutionary statement to the Jews?
    The Jews were taxed for the support of their priests and the Gentiles paid fees.

36. What is the result of entering into a common life with your teacher?
    A strong bond of family and love, encouragement and support. Sharing in the joy of cultivating and harvesting kingdom fruit.

37. Read 1 Corinthians 9:9-14. Was God concerned with the oxen?
    No.

38. With what attitude should you plow?
    With hope.

39. And if you thresh?
    In hope, to be a partaker of hope.

40. Is it a sin or greediness to partake of the material fruit if you have sown spiritual seeds?
    No.

41. What has the Lord commanded in verse 14?
    Those who preach the Gospel should live from and be supported by the Gospel.

42. What must you be careful to NOT do in this circumstance?
    To use your position for manipulative and ill means for filthy lucre.

43. Read Galatians 6:7-8. What are you NOT to be?
    KJV - Deceived.
    SE - Fooled.
    LB - Misled.

44. Is it possible to trick God?
    No. Why not?
    Whatever a man plants is what he will harvest.

45. What kind of seeds does one plant to harvest a crop of weeds and destruction?
    Selfishness and evil.

46. What does the Living Bible say he will reap a harvest of?
    Spiritual decay and death.

47. Read Romans 8:13. What is the harvest if you sow to the Spirit?
Everlasting life.

48. Using the list from Galatians 5:19-21, list some examples of "sowing to the flesh."
Adultery, idolatry, lewdness, hatred, jealousy, wrath, contentions, and selfish ambition.

49. List again the fruit of the Spirit (Galatians 5:22-23).
Love, joy, peace, longsuffering, gentleness, goodness, faith, meekness, and temperance.

50. Read Galatians 6:9. How does Paul describe an active faith? (Compare Commentary Notes and Romans 2:7)
   a. It sows to the Spirit.
   b. It manifests in well doing.
   c. It reaps an everlasting harvest.

51. What are we promised if we don't give up?
A good harvest.

52. Read Colossians 3:17, 23-23. What is our reward for being a God-pleaser instead of a man-pleaser?
The reward of the inheritance.

53. James 1:4 (AMP) – *"But let endurance and steadfastness and patience have full play and do a thorough work, so that you may be [people] perfectly and fully developed [with no defects], lacking in nothing."* What three things must you allow to have "full-play" and do a thorough work in you?
   1. Endurance.
   2. Steadfastness.
   3. Patience.

54. Read Galatians 6:10. Since we know that we will reap a harvest for our efforts (verse 9), what are we exhorted to do?
Do good to all.

55. When is it we are "to do good unto all men"?
Every time we get an opportunity.

56. Although we are to do good unto all men, where should we begin our service?
In the household of faith, the family of believers.

57. Are we to wait for opportunities to come knocking? (See Commentary Notes)
No, we are to look for opportunities to do good to others.

58. Read Galatians 6:11. What was Paul trying to emphasize to the Galatians with his "bold scrawls"?
The immense importance of his letter to them.

59. Read Galatians 6:12. Why was it the Judaizers acted deceptively in regards to the gospel of Jesus Christ?
    LB a. **So they can be popular.**
    b. **To avoid the persecution that comes with faith in Christ.**
    TM a. **It was an easy way to look good before others.**
    b. **They lacked the courage to live a faith that shares Christ's sufferings and death.**

60. Read Galatians 2:19-20. In order to live, with Whom do you have to be crucified?
With Christ.

61. If you are crucified with Christ, do you also share in His sufferings?
Yes.

62. Read Galatians 6:12-13. Even though the Judaizers professed Christ with their lips, what exposed their falsity and deceitfulness?
Their actions didn't line up with their words, and they were not truly willing to suffer persecution for following the message of the cross.

63. Read John 14:21 and 1 John 3:23. How can you tell if someone truly loves Christ?
They will obey the Lord's commandments, which are to believe on Jesus and to love one another.

64. Read Galatians 6:13. Did those who were already circumcised keep the Law?
No.

65. Why, then, did they require others to keep the Law through circumcision?
So that they could boast of their success in recruiting others to join them in their beliefs.

66. Read Matthew 5:17 and Romans 8:3-4 (NKJV). Who was the only one who could fulfill the Law?
Jesus.

67. Read John 15:13, Romans 13:8-10, and Galatians 5:14. How was the Law fulfilled?
By Jesus laying down His life because of His great love for us.

68. Read Galatians 6:14 and Ephesians 2:8-9. Why did God save us by grace and not by our works?
So that no man could boast that he could save himself by his works.

69. Read Romans 3:23-28. According to verse 23, what is man "guilty" of?
    a. Sinning.
    b. Falling short of the glory of God.

70. Read Romans 5:8. Since we couldn't save ourselves, what did God do for us?
    He sent forth His Son, Jesus, to die for us while we were still sinners.

71. Read Romans 3:27. Where is boasting then?
    It is excluded.

72. Read Romans 3:28. What can we therefore conclude?
    Man is justified by faith apart from the Law.

73. Read Galatians 6:14. What is the only thing we should boast about?
    The cross of our Lord Jesus Christ.

74. From what three things does Galatians 6:14 in The Message say the cross has set us free?
    a. We are crucified in relation to the world.
    b. We are free from the stifling atmosphere of pleasing others.
    c. From fitting into the patterns that the world dictates.

75. Read Galatians 1:10. Can you successfully be a man-pleaser first, and a God-pleaser at the same time?
    No.

76. Read Galatians 6:15. What is the important thing in your life with Christ? (LB)
    That we have been changed into new and different people.

77. Can you accomplish this by altering outside appearances?
    No.

78. Read Galatians 6:15. How does The Message describe what the "central issue" is?
    "It is what God is doing, and He is creating something totally new, a free life."

79. Read 2 Corinthians 5:17. If you are in Christ, what is your true identity?
    I am a new creation.

80. What has happened to your old identity?
    It has passed away.

81. Read Colossians 3:10. How can you tell if someone is a "new man"?
    He is renewed in knowledge, that is, his brand-new nature is continually being renewed as he learns more and more about Christ, who created this new nature within him.

82. Read Galatians 6:16. What will be the result if you walk out your salvation as a "new creature"?
God's mercy and peace will be upon you.

83. Read Romans 9:6-7 and 2:28-29. Who are the Israel of God?
Those who are circumcised in the heart. These are the children of promise.

84. Read Galatians 3:26, 29 and 4:28. Who are the children of the promise?
We are, by faith in Christ Jesus.

85. Read Galatians 6:17. Was Paul telling the Galatians to not bother him with their troubles anymore?
No.

86. Then what do you think he is talking about?
To stop trying to get him to turn from the Gospel of truth of peace and grace back over into legalism.

87. Why is it Paul is able to stand so strongly against the persecution of the Judaizers?" (SE)
Because he knows to Whom he belongs.

88. When you come to the fullness of the revelation of whom you belong, how will that change your current walk with the Lord?
No one will be able to trouble you and try to persuade you back into the clutches of sin and death.

89. Read 2 Timothy 3:12. Who are they who are suffering persecution for Christ?
Those who are truly godly.

90. Read Galatians 6:18. What is Paul's final exhortation?
That the grace of our Lord be with you.

91. Why did he pray for "grace" to be upon them?
Because they were in danger of forsaking grace for legalism.

92. How does The Message paraphrase this verse?
May what Jesus gives freely be deeply and personally yours.